Wordplay

THE PHILOSOPHY, ART, &

SCIENCE OF AMBIGRAMS

John Langdon

wordplay

BROADWAY BOOKS

NEW YORK

BROADWAY

For permissions credits, see page 203.

First Broadway Books edition published 2005

Library of Congress Cataloging-in-Publication Data

Langdon, John, 1946–
Wordplay: the philosophy, art, and science of ambigrams / John Langdon. — 1st ed.
p. cm.
"A previous edition of this book was published in 1992
by Harcourt, Brace Javonovich"—T.p. verso.
1. Calligraphy. 2. Play on words. 3. Ambiguity. I. Title

Z43.L259 2005
745.6'1—dc22
2005046973

ISBN 0-7679-2075-9

3   5   7   9   10   8   6   4   2

CONTENTS

Philosophy is written in this grand book—
I mean the universe—which stands
continually open to our gaze, but it cannot
be understood unless one first learns to
comprehend the language and interpret
the characters in which it is written.

—*Il Saggiatore*, Galileo Galilei

"...the books are something like our books,
only the words go the wrong way..."

—Through the Looking Glass, Lewis Carroll

Foreword

If you've not yet experienced the artwork of John Langdon, you're in for a treat. A brilliant alchemist of symbols and language, John dissolves everyday icons, words, and ideas . . . reconstituting them with astonishing results. I'll never forget seeing John's art for the first time. One evening in 1993, my father (a math teacher who delights in word play) excitedly called me into his study to show me what he called "an utterly ingenious piece of art." I hurried in, expecting to see some impossible Escher or baffling Dalí. To my disappointment, the masterpiece appeared to be nothing more than a single word—*Philosophy*—rendered in an ornate, cursive script.

"Philosophy?" I said to my Dad. "So what?"

With a patient smile, my father rotated the word 180 degrees . . . turning it upside down.

Such was my introduction to John Langdon's *Wordplay*—his magical universe of symmetry and illusion. I became an instant fan. Like a composer who transforms and recapitulates a symphonic theme, John takes familiar words and symbols, ingeniously skewing, twisting, and re-arranging them so he can "re-present" them in a new light. This book (which, by the way, you are now reading upside down) is both playful and profound . . . both witty and reflective. John's accompanying text is a philosophy in itself . . . subtle, insightful, and inspirational. If you're like me, you'll find yourself opening this book over and over . . . amazed as new perspectives unveil themselves with each fresh exploration. I leave you now in the hands of an artist who does with words what mere authors can only dream. Without further ado, I urge you . . . rotate this book once again, and dive into John Langdon's *Wordplay*—a world where everything is exactly as it seems . . . and also otherwise.

Dan Brown

Philosophy

Introduction

It's a lot harder, when you're young, to see where you're going than it is, when you're older, to see where you've been. Decades back, the landscape was littered with dots. I now see which ones are connected.

By way of heredity, I carry with me a passion for language, and a strong affinity for visual art. My various job titles—logo designer, typographic designer, lettering artist, ambigram artist, and word artist—therefore make a lot of sense. I grew up with most of the cultural influences of my "baby boom" generation, but with a unique set of circumstances all my own. Somewhere in that combination of factors, I'd imagine, are the reasons why I have always been interested in what things, ideas, and, in particular, words look like from unorthodox points of view. My contrarian mind may have been responsible for my resistance to the education I was offered, thus necessitating that I educate myself in ways that were designed—by me, obviously—just for me.

However it evolved, I have a deep need to understand meanings and origins—of words especially, but the meanings and origins of ideas, cultural and scientific, as well. My method involves little research and academic study; it is, for the most part, inductive and intuitive, and based heavily on analogy: this letter looks like that letter, this symbol resembles another, this concept seems to parallel that one.

The most meaningful moment in this alternative education was my first encounter with the yin/yang symbol. I was strongly moved by what seems to have been an almost immediate understanding of its implications. Rather than seek out what I could read about Taoism (the ancient Chinese philosophy that the symbol represents), I began to make yin and yang the object of my frequent graphic meditations and explorations—deconstructing and reconstructing the symbol itself, and any idea that seemed related to it.

I am very fortunate to have found a way for "being me" to be my career. No career counselor could ever have laid out a plan by which I could become who I am, doing what I do. There has never been a want ad for an ambigram artist. It could only happen by following my nose, my instincts, and my heart, letting the various choices and influences—serendipitous and purposeful—accumulate until they all added up to something. Something that eventually even had a name.

This book will give you, appropriately enough, a number of different vantage points from which to ponder ambigrams. The heart of the book is a group of ambigrams, thematically related by way of their significance in Western science, Eastern philosophy, or, most often, both. Each is accompanied by a short essay that may explore the meaning of the word, its etymology, its significance in cultural history, and why it's a natural candidate for ambigrammatic presentation. On the other hand, the occasional essay will simply be a lighthearted diversion intended to have as much fun with wordplay as possible.

Although *Wordplay* is a much more serious book than its title might suggest, play is a significant part of my creative process. It is often through play that we make unexpected discoveries; indeed it was by way of play that I discovered the rabbit hole to the wonderland of ambigrams, and play is the first stage in the development of each one.

Later, I'll relate the full history of my ambigrams from way back somewhere almost to the day this manuscript was completed. The history section will attempt to show how various symbols, artists, art movements, and trends in popular culture had significant influences on me, and how they eventually led to the invention, discovery, and development of my ambigrams. This section will reveal how the first edition of *Wordplay* came to the attention of Dan Brown, and how ambigrams found their way into his wonderful best-selling novel, *Angels & Demons*. Since *A&D* has taken my ambigrams to the far corners of the world, I have had requests for commissioned ambigram designs from many people and places. I have greatly enjoyed working on those, and I've included a number of my favorites in this section.

I conclude with a section called "How a Word Becomes an Ambigram," in which I try to explain each step from the earliest notion, through all the playful exploration and un-playful (but still enjoyable) drawing—involving innumerable tiny refinements—to the processes involved in creating an ambigram's final artwork.

Ultimately this is a book of a personal philosophy—one inspired by a symbol that originated in the philosophy of a culture from long ago and far away. The ideas contained in *Wordplay* were developed over a period of about twenty years, paralleling the development of my ambigrams. The ambigrams have not led me to the philosophy. Rather, they are the natural result of the philosophy coming to rest in the mind of an artist who loves words.

Discovering the Tao

The first time I saw the yin and yang symbol was one of those moments that become permanent mental photographs. I didn't know back in 1966 what lay beyond the door, but it is now clear that a door had opened for me. Yin and yang made a deep and immediate impression—an impression I was aware of somewhere between my nervous system and the source of my emotions, but would have been hard pressed to identify or describe out loud. If I had said anything, I might have quoted the introduction to the 1960s TV program Ben Casey: "Man . . . woman . . . birth . . . death . . . infinity . . . ," followed perhaps by "summer, winter, hot, cold, north, south, on, off, up, down," and so on. Although it would be several years before I ever heard of Taoism, the ancient Chinese philosophy from which yin and yang originates, I seem to have subconsciously sensed that the symbol's simple representation of polarized opposites and harmonious complements applied perfectly to most of the major forces inherent in our existence.

I pondered the yin and yang symbol and fooled around with it graphically for years, at first unaware of the interest in Eastern thought that was to grow steadily in popularity through the ensuing decades. After seeing parts of this book in its early stages, a young physics student

DISCOVERING

wrote to me: "Taoist imagery of interaction and of a natural, flowing, universal holism is becoming more and more infused into our consciousness. Such ideas have been a latent part of our psyche for centuries. Their lineage can be traced, almost directly, from the Renaissance hermeticists, to the alchemists and early scientists, through writers such as Eliot and Joyce, and finally into aspects of our own popular culture."

The sixties' pop culture included a significant amount of interest in Eastern thought, which has since filtered into many more mainstream facets of Western culture.

In the same way that the cross could be thought of as a logo for Christianity and the Star of David as a logo for Judaism, the yin and yang symbol is a logo for Taoism. As such, it is one of the best logos ever designed. A logo should communicate, in as simple and efficient a form as possible, a maximum of information about the entity it represents. And by the time I began to read about Taoism, I found to my amazement that I had already inferred virtually all that I was reading, simply by applying the ideas of polarized opposites and harmonious complements to a seemingly infinite number of situations that exist in our lives and in the workings of the universe. This, I learned, is quite appropriate to Taoism, a basic tenet of which holds that each person should find his own way. In the words of Lao-tzu, "Without leaving my house, I [can] know the whole universe."

It seems likely that Taoism developed in much the same way as the physical sciences did—through observation of the world around us. Sir Isaac Newton is perhaps best known for his third law, which states that "for every action, there is opposed an equal and opposite reaction." The yin and yang symbol may as well have been designed to illustrate that idea. In his letter to me, the physics student also said, "Science has directly encountered [the yin/yang] theme in the study of dynamical systems, popularly termed 'chaos theory.' Chaotic behavior . . . is dependent on a feedback mechanism, in which each of several factors interacts to determine the value of the others. It can be said that fractals are none other than microscopic images, resolvable to infinite but never ultimate detail, of the interaction between yin and yang." "Chaos" may not be the best name for this relatively new area of scientific study. The subjects of its interest have indeed appeared to be chaotic for centuries, but as they begin to be understood, they exhibit instead a different kind of order—one that has eluded classical scientific methods. Yin-and-yang-like relationships are beginning to emerge between, for example, order and disorder, and stability and instability.

I began to investigate other basic scientific principles and often found either visual representations of data, such as the "normal bell curve," or descriptions of visible physical phenomena, like wave patterns. For instance, not only does a path worn by a random sampling of a population walking across an open area of grass describe a "path" of least resistance, but its depression into the earth is virtually a normal distribution curve, albeit an inverted one, caused by the majority of people walking down the middle of it. The spiral is frequently found in patterns that nature creates, from the microscopic DNA helix, through snail shells and sunflowers, to galaxies thousands of light-years across. Often the shapes and proportions of these spirals mathematically follow the Fibonacci series: 1, 1, 2, 3, 5, 8, 13, 21, etc. Wavelengths seem similar to a series of normal distribution curves, and the infinity symbol could be seen as two normal bell curves curled around and linked to complete a circuit. They all seem graphically, philosophically, and scientifically related to one another *and* to the yin and yang symbol. They all appealed to me in the same way that yin and yang had—as simple and beautiful shapes that represented basic and powerful universal principles. Naturally, the names of these symbols and concepts became candidates for word designs that might illuminate the ideas they represent and demonstrate their relationships to the overriding yin and yang principle. And so they became ambigrams.

The yin/yang principle was, for many years, a dominant focus of my private thinking and my personal development. It has in recent years become less an object of my meditations, and more an underlying principle of how I see the world.

Yin and Yang

In the act of creation, a man brings together two facets of reality and, by discovering a likeness between them, makes them one.

Science and Human Values, Jacob Bronowski

Taoism is an ancient Chinese philosophy that is based on the observation that the universe is a dynamic system driven by the interplay of opposing and complementary forces. The yin and yang symbol represents that system with elegant effectiveness. The black yin shape synthesizes the feminine principle: darkness, inwardness, yielding, and the unknown; the white yang represents the masculine principle: light, protrusion, aggressiveness, and the overt.

Since none of these characteristics could exist without its counterpart, each is necessarily an aspect of the other. To be more accurate, each yin and each yang is an integral aspect or part of a greater whole: "yinandyang"—or the Tao.

The Tao (pronounced "dow") can be an elusive concept. Indeed, the predominant piece of Taoist literature, the *Tao Te Ching*, begins with "The tao that can be told is not the eternal Tao. The name that can be named is not the eternal Name." This seems to parallel imponderables and proscriptions in other spiritual traditions. We obviously need to acknowledge that there is something way, way beyond our ability to understand. The word *Tao* is perhaps best understood as "the way" or "the path." Those definitions can be thought of as meaning "the way" the universe works, and "the path" we would choose to live in harmony with the way of the universe around us.

Yin and yang looks fluid, and it is, in fact, quite flexible. Taking it to an extreme, but a thought-provoking point of view, philosopher Alan Watts said that at times he felt that he was yang and the entire rest of the universe was yin.

The shapes of the yin and the yang not only resemble droplets of liquid, but they aptly describe the ebb and flow of various fluid rhythms, in both time and space. As a pendulum changes its course when it has reached the extreme point of its swing in one direction, so yang begins at a tiny point where yin reaches its greatest width. Immediately following summer's "longest day of the year," the amount of daily darkness begins, imperceptibly perhaps, to move back toward winter. In other words, a characteristic symptom of winter can first be detected in midsummer. How far can you walk into the woods? Only halfway. After that, you're walking out.

Adjacent to the point where yang begins, in the middle of the maximum width of yin, is a dot of white. This signifies the idea that the very act of reaching a maximum point creates the seed (as it's often described) of an opposite reaction. It's as if, in its final push to expand to its maximum, yin has ruptured itself, creating a small gap. It's two centimeters dilated and about to give birth—to yang.

Another way of looking at this idea would demonstrate that in a

HARMONIOUS COMPLEMENTS

Ying & Yang

POLARIZED
OPPOSITES

I created a yin/yang sphere and hung it from the ceiling. Most of the time, as it slowly revolves in the air currents of the room, either yin or yang appears to dominate. The surface of that sphere is exactly half white and half black, but only rarely does it appear that way.

Yin/Yang Sphere. Styrofoam, plaster, enamel, 1985.

complementary relationship between entities, the total elimination of one by the other is impossible. Because it is light that creates darkness, in the form of shadows, light cannot ever do away with all darkness. Unless perhaps someday—and it would be day!—all mass is converted to light energy. In a hypothetical relationship, with one species feeding only on one other, it would be impossible for the predator species to devour all of its prey. As the population of the prey dwindled to the point where the members of the predator species could not all be fed, the predators would begin to die off. The trend would reverse, and soon the population of the prey species could begin to increase. An all-and-nothing relationship can be approached, but yin and yang's natural tendency toward balance prevents it from being achieved.

While the complementary "halves" of such relationships may not always appear to be equal, eventually most of them do turn out that way. Day and night are equal amounts of time only twice a year, at the equinoxes. But over the course of a year, every place on earth has day and night half of the time. Seeing Taoist balance often requires that the viewer step back, in either space or time, and take a longer view.

Yin and yang can function as a graph in which such complementary relationships are described. Much of the time the complementary opposites exist in a dominant and subordinate relationship. But yin and yang is never static.

Sociological research may show a majority point of view continuing to grow in popularity, but eventually the human instinct for individuality will react and a countermovement will arise. The social upheaval of the sixties was in direct response not only to the Vietnam War, the

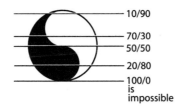

10/90
70/30
50/50
20/80
100/0
is
impossible

One of the axiomatic truths of yin and yang is that you can't have one without the other. Attempting to do the impossible is usually a stimulating exercise, so I decided to try. The resulting image, the yin chasing its tail, is yin, alone . . . period. The period, of course, has fallen from its position in the yang area, demonstrating that yang is there, as always, just not where you thought it would be. All the area beyond, as well as the area enclosed by the yin shape, is yang. When you have just yin, then everything else is yang, like Alan Watts's egocentric fantasy. It's a painting about the amusing and ironic way that the painting failed to achieve its purpose.

overt oppression of African-Americans, and the thinly veiled oppression of women, but also to the widespread acceptance of the fifties' postwar values. Conformity, convenience, and anticommunism were stretched so far over all aspects of American society that they became shallow and transparent. The larger the balloon grows, the more vulnerable it becomes. Oppression always breeds rebellion. So natural is this instinct that for the most part, things tend not to shift to extremes. The need for relative stability and balance usually keeps things hovering in a range near the center, but the greater the trend in one direction, the more extreme the response will be.

Yin and yang represents nature's ability to keep things in balance in a constantly shifting process of give and take.

Yin, Period. Oil on canvas, 1997.

Philosophy, Art, & Science

The search for truth will continue as long as there are human beings with curiosity. It will be pursued forever and never attained. This is due to the attitudes and working processes of those whose mission it is to define truth: philosophers, artists, and scientists.

The processes of philosophy require that strict logic be adhered to, and that conventions of argument be followed. For example, if A is true, then it must follow that B is also true. Or since A and B are true, then C cannot be true. A philosophical idea must be supported by logic and is likely to be subjected to challenge from another logical construct, another point of view. In general, philosophers do not attempt to establish immutable truths. Philosophers gain respect and gather adherents, knowing full well that they may, in time, lose both. The field seems to accept that there will always be another person with a new approach to "The Truth." The word *philosophy* does not mean a love of, or a knowledge of, truth. Rather it means "a love of wisdom"—having the capacity to ponder truths. In other words, it's not whether you win or lose, it's how smart a game you play.

The root of the word *science*, on the other hand, is the Latin word "to know." Historically, science has tried to reach conclusions. But the stan-

THREE VOCATIONS
WITH ONE GOAL: TO
ESTABLISH TRUTHS
ABOUT OURSELVES
AND THE COSMOS

Philosophy Art & Science

THE THREE POINTS
OF AN EQUILATERAL
TRIANGLE; AS UNA-
LIKE AS THE THREE
PRIMARY COLORS

dards for acceptance are much more rigorous. Scientists attempt to ascertain their truths through hypothesis, experiment, deduction, and proof. A hypothesis often meets its ultimate test in the practice of disproof. It may be supported by any number of experiments, but if it can be disproved as well, it cannot be thought of as a truth, no matter how logical it may seem.

When a hypothesis has been proved and cannot be disproved, it may be thought of as being true, for the time being, at least. Strong hypotheses, supported by successful experiments, can build a "theory"—an interlocking set of laws that explain certain phenomena. When verified, hypotheses become theories—and are accepted as "provisionally true." Einstein's hypotheses regarding space and time have been borne out many times in the past several decades, so they have become known as "The Theory of Relativity." But science is always willing to replace "truths" with newer "truths."

Testing each new "truth" exposes new information, which raises new questions, and thereby engenders new hypotheses. With the demands made upon scientific process and the acceptance that truths may be only temporary, we see once again that Ultimate Truths are something of a Holy Grail—a carrot at the end of the stick. As Jacob Bronowski says, in *Science and Human Values,* "Science is not a mechanism but a human progress, and not a set of findings but the search for them."

Completing the equilateral triangle of truth seekers are the artists. Bronowski goes on: "The creative act is alike in art as in science; but it cannot be identical in the two; there must be a difference as well as a likeness . . . the artist in his creation surely has open to him a dimension of freedom which is closed to the scientist." Whereas philosophers are

MAY ALLOW
OR REQUIRE
LOOKING AT
IDEAS FROM
BOTH SIDES.

Philosophy

IS A SCIENCE
DEFINED AS
THE PURSUIT,
STUDY & LOVE
OF WISDOM.

guided and constrained by logic, and scientists are careful to use strict controls to assure the accuracy of their data and findings, artists are free to approach truths by any path with no expectation of following what was done before. Artists can hardly expect *not* to follow, as it is too late to precede, but they try not to be led, at least. They often proceed by way of a synthesizing process, looking not to the recent past but to a more distant antecedent to blend with their own very current ideas. Thus the viewer looks at something familiar in a completely different way. This is the case with the ambigrams in this book: they pull together ancient philosophies, traditional science, and unorthodox lettering design. Their goal is to engender a new point of view toward words that may have long been familiar.

Bronowski's philosophy brings the separate fields of science and art together: "Science is nothing else than the search to discover unity in the wild variety of nature—or more exactly, in the variety of our experience." Quoting Samuel Taylor Coleridge's definition of beauty, "unity in variety," Bronowski says, "The arts are the same search. . . . Each in its own way looks for likenesses within the variety of human experience." Describing science as a creative endeavor, he says, "In the act of creation, a man brings together two facets of reality and, by discovering a likeness between them, makes them one. This act is the same in Leonardo, in Keats and in Einstein. And the spectator who is moved by the finished work of art or the scientific theory re-lives the same discovery; his appreciation also is a re-creation."

In art, the well-worn path is to be avoided lest the product be considered craft. But the goal of art has never been to *establish* truth, only to provide more views of it. Somewhere on Earth an artist produces an-

"THE WHOLE OF SCIENCE IS
NOTHING MORE THAN A RE-
FINEMENT OF EVERYDAY
THINKING." ALBERT EINSTEIN

science

"ALL THAT SCIENCE CAN
ACHIEVE IS A PERFECT
KNOWLEDGE AND A PER-
FECT UNDERSTANDING
OF THE ACTION OF NATU-
RAL AND MORAL FORCES."
*HERMANN LUDWIG FER-
DINAND VON HELMHOLTZ*

other glimpse at reality every minute, so the process will never be complete. In the visual arts, as in science, there will always be another way of looking at things.

In philosophy, science, and art, it is the process that is important. The processes provide us with temporary truths which, since each moment of reality is only temporary itself, ought to be satisfactory for the time being. All that can really be done is to record and organize human experience. But that's all right— it gives artists, scientists, and philosophers something to do.

That's exactly how the search for truth is supposed to work. You see something and then you try everything you can think of to make it go away; you turn it inside out and upside down, and push on it from every possible angle. If it's still there, maybe you've got something.

The Universe and the Teacup: The Mathematics of Truth and Beauty, K. C. Cole

Hypothesis/Thesis/ Antithesis/Synthesis

A hypothesis is an idea that may explain a phenomenon but has not been tested to determine its value. Dictionaries define *thesis* as a proposition, an affirmation, and a postulate, essentially a hypothesis that is being presented for testing. *Antithesis* is defined as a contrast, an opposition, a contrary, a point of view to challenge the hypothesis. These definitions are familiar in academic circles, and often used to describe aspects of debate. For instance—Thesis: The sun is the source of all life. Antithesis: God is the giver of all life.

From my point of view, the ideal outcome of a debate is not the triumph of one side over the other, but the emergence of a third point of view in which both the thesis and the antithesis have been brought into harmony. Synthesis: God is the sun. The sun is God.

The word *thesis* is seldom heard outside of an academic arena, but it is not uncommon to hear someone say that one thing is the "antithesis" of another: "Science is the antithesis of art," "The antithesis of love is hate," and more. While these examples may themselves be fodder for debate, they represent our instinctive need to define and understand one thing in terms of another. Every yin is the antithesis of a complementary yang. In a debate, as in the thesis/antithesis ring, each thesis in a series of theses can be met and countered by an anti-thesis.

This opposition between thesis and antithesis could be graphically represented by a black rectangle and a white rectangle of equal size adjacent to each other. But this describes a static situation in which the tension inherent in the relationship is never resolved.

Like participants in many arguments, neither has any effect on the other. There could be a winner or loser, but no give and take. There is nothing learned or agreed upon—in short, there is no synthesis.

Synthesis is a combination of separate elements fashioned into a (synthetic) whole new entity. But a blend of the two ingredients would seldom be a satisfactory synthesis. The only way we could picture a combination of the black and white rectangles above would be as something that, in a debate, would look pretty disappointing from both vantage points: gray—a compromise, and both sides *have* been compromised.

But when the opposites of thesis and antithesis are pictured as yin and as yang, however, they fit together in a very satisfying composite whole, with each side retaining its character and integrity.

synthesis

A COMBINATION OF ELEMENTS
FROM BOTH THE THESIS...

AND THE ANTITHESIS,
RESULTING IN AN IDEAL WHOLE.

Art is the antithesis of science. They are fundamentally different. The scientific method proceeds from the left hemisphere of the brain, moving methodically, each step based upon the data from the preceding step. Art emanates from the right hemisphere and, not constrained by logic, is propelled by intuition and imaginative association. Yet while their individual characteristics vary greatly, art and science are essentially the same. Each is a process involving the observation of phenomena in order to describe and understand the world around us.

Thesis: art. Antithesis: science. Synthesis: Da Vinci.

Thesis: art.   **Antithesis: science.**   **Synthesis: Da Vinci.**

Theory

Among the more interesting challenges that arise in the wordplay arena is taking differing meanings of the same word and tracing them back to a common root. It is a rewarding process of synthesis—a reuniting of broken parts. The word *theory* has proven to be one of the most challenging of all, perhaps because it emerges in the effort to answer the tricky question, "What is truth?" which, as we have seen, can never be conclusively established.

The word *theory* is derived from a Greek word that means "viewing." And the divergent ways in which scientists and the general public seem to view this word are as different as black and white. Seeing words and ideas from different points of view is the entire raison d'être of this book, of course, and the connotations and denotations of *theory* are yet another linguistic yin and yang. In the way we commonly use the word, it could be synonymous with speculation or conjecture—a hunch or a guess. For scientists, a stricter denotation applies: a theory is an idea that *can* be accepted as truth, or *is* accepted as "provisionally true." The chain connecting the two meanings is forged of rather ethereal links: "Ultimate Truth," "Truth," "truth," "reality," "temporary truth," "provisional truth," all of which might seem to be pretty similar, but it's their differences that make the chain both possible and tenuous.

RELATIVITY

A scientist begins with an educated guess called a hypothesis, the validity of which is tested by experimentation. In the course of this process, certain principles may emerge that ultimately result in a system of laws, which, in turn, explains the phenomena in question. That organized network of principles or set of laws is called a theory. If experimentation verifies the hypothesis, a theory is accepted as being valid. For example, quantum theory and the theory of relativity are now considered to be valid. They have been supported by subsequent findings and have not been disproved. Therefore they are accepted as accurate descriptions of various aspects of reality.

Here comes the gray area. One reason a "true" theory is not considered to be "The Truth" is the fact that it has not been tested in every place and time in the universe. As an example, the passage of time was assumed to be uniform until Einstein's relativity theory proved that earthly time and time measured in a spaceship would not match up. Newton's laws of motion seemed to be immutable until it was discovered that they simply aren't in effect in the subatomic realm. Still, we hold on to our dependence on clocks, and continue to rely on the effectiveness of Newton's laws, as long as we're here on Earth in a supra-atomic reality. Scientists hold open the possibility that ideas may be modified, supplanted, or disproved by discoveries not yet made. It is this cautious allowance that leads to the more common use of the word *theory*.

Whereas most people assume that there is a definite reality out there that is patiently waiting to have all of its aspects understood, scientists are more likely to accept the notion of an infinite reality, one that will always have more mysteries and engender more questions. The truths of

A SET OF LAWS
WHICH EXPLAIN
WHAT DOES NOT
EXIST, BUT CAN BE
UNDERSTOOD.

A SYSTEMATIC
EXPLANATION
FOR THAT WHICH
EXISTS, & YET ISN'T
UNDERSTOOD.

yesteryear—the Earth is flat, the Earth is the center of the cosmos, and so forth—are no longer true. Each was supported in its day by observation. Making sense of our experiences is what theories and "truth" are all about. Aided by what currently seems like incredible technology, we believe that our observations are much more sensitive these days. The practice of science is the constant refinement of our observations. In the future we'll know more about virtually everything as technology continues to allow for more powerful, accurate and sensitive observation.

This leads to another point of confusion in the use of the word *theory.* Since scientists accept the idea that there is a difference between theoretical reality and observed reality, a theory is considered to represent an ideal state. This is because no study can claim to have examined *all* the aspects of any given situation. Once a modus operandi for a given phenomenon has been developed, it can be encoded in a formula that smoothes off the rough edges of the reality. Since those rough edges actually exist, the formula represents the way things work in an ideal state—"in theory." *Theory* describes the accurate and truthful formula. Einstein put it this way: "As far as the laws of mathematics refer to reality, they are not certain, and as far as they are certain, they do not refer to reality."

Scientists recognize that there is more "reality" than our technology can currently measure. But they are willing to hope and presume, for the time being, that since their theories have held up to date, any future refinements will continue to support them. This is an idealistic attitude, and scientists know that reality *may* prove to be different. We don't often think of scientists as being idealistic, but in this regard, they must be. Idealists are commonly thought to be out of touch with reality, and in common usage, an "ideal" is taken to be something that does *not* exist.

Theories dance around, encircling the way things work. They describe what does not exist—an ideal—so that we can understand things. They define what does exist—"reality"—despite the fact that all its aspects are not and cannot ever be known. Here's the crux of the matter: theories describe not the way things work as much as our *understanding* of how they work.

Ambiguity

In John Godfrey Saxe's well-known poem "The Blind Men and the Elephant," the six blind men of Indostan all went to learn what an elephant was like. Each approached the beast from a different direction and felt in turn the elephant's side, its tusk, its trunk, its leg, its ear, and its tail. Relating their experiences to what was familiar to them, the six compared the elephant to, respectively, a wall, a spear, a snake, a tree, a fan, and a rope. The poem ends:

> *And so these men of Indostan*
> *Disputed loud and long,*
> *Each in his own opinion*
> *Exceeding stiff and strong,*
> *Though each was partly in the right,*
> *And all were in the wrong!*

If there are ten witnesses to a traffic accident or a crime, they'll often provide ten differing accounts—none of which may be incorrect. When I imagine this situation, I picture the witnesses spread randomly around a circle with the incident taking place in the middle. Their accounts are transcribed from their memories as if they were each describing a pho-

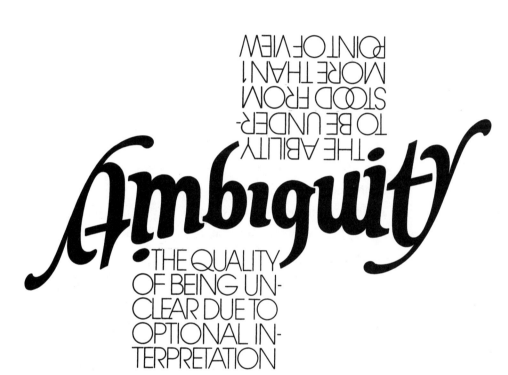

Ambiguity

THE ABILITY TO BE UNDER-STOOD FROM MORE THAN 1 POINT OF VIEW.

THE QUALITY OF BEING UN-CLEAR DUE TO OPTIONAL IN-TERPRETATION

tograph they had taken at the same moment. If they had, each photograph would, of course, be a two-dimensional representation of the scene from one of several points of view. If all the "photographs" were blended into a composite, a more three-dimensional, and therefore more "real," picture would result. We sometimes refer to that picture as "reality" or "truth." Cubist painters often painted different, overlapping views of the same object—and argued that they were providing a more "real" representation of reality than the "realistic" images of traditional painting—or than images coming from the relatively new field of photography. (Eventually photography would use the same approach to create a holographic image.)

We commonly use the word *ambiguity* to describe a situation that is hard to understand; but that's because the situation *can* be understood from more than one point of view. Given the examples above, it would be fair to say that every situation—all reality—is ambiguous. Most of us respond to ambiguities and cubist paintings in the same way. We don't understand them, so we retreat from them. Logically, though, it would seem that the more ambiguity there is, the more accurate the description of reality can be. When we hold fast to our single, individual point of view, we don't have the benefit of the other points of view. If we really want to understand the world around us, we should embrace ambiguity and always try to see a situation from as many different points of view as possible.

Generally, people don't want to have to see things from other points of view. It's so much easier to live with our two-dimensional photographs. And yet, ambiguity is actually built into our physical makeup so that we *can* understand our surroundings. Each of our two eyes sees a slightly different image. The brain takes these two images and synthesizes them into a single picture, one of the important features of which is the perception of depth, and this would not be the case were we to have but one eye. This phenomenon has been dramatically demonstrated over the past several generations through stereopticons, Viewmasters and 3-D movie glasses. In each of these, two different two-dimensional images seen separately by two eyes take on the appearance of a single three-dimensional reality.

Reality is ambiguous. Ambiguity is synthesis. The problem and the solution are one.

All photos are accurate. None of them is the truth.

—Richard Avedon

Reality

Have you ever been in a conversation when, after you've expressed your point of view, someone says, "In a situation like this, you really need to be more realistic"? Or maybe, "Well, I'm impressed by your idealism, but I'm a realist." My response (thought, more often than said) is "So who gave you the key to the clubhouse and the secret handshake?" People use the word *reality* as if it had a set of finite dimensions, a weight, a molecular structure, and an atomic number (that some *special* people have on their speed dial).

Many fish see their environment through something like a fish-eye lens . . . or two. Is their idea of reality distorted? Or is ours? Can the answer possibly be neither? Or both? The eyes of some insects have a thousand lenses or more. There are animals that can see colors in the ultraviolet and infrared parts of the spectrum. There are sounds beyond our range of hearing, and languages without words for certain colors. Are we arrogant enough to believe that what we experience is reality and what other individuals or species experience is something other than that? The evidence suggests that each of us experiences a different "reality"—and one that is well matched to our survival needs.

On a day-to-day basis, of course, we're able to move though the day in a pretty orderly way, because our assumptions about our environ-

REALITY
realityrealityrealityrealityrealityrealityrealityrealityrealityreality

ment are supported by our experiences. Quantum physics might like to introduce a good deal more uncertainty to our lives, but up here where we live, it's still a pretty dependable Newtonian world (thank goodness). Nevertheless, there's no doubt that many of the conflicts we experience—personally, culturally, internationally—are only understandable if we allow for the idea that people see things differently. My wife and I had a car that I always referred to as green, while she was quite certain that it was blue. We were both quite certain of what color the car was. Would it make any sense to say that one of us was wrong?

Reality is as we perceive it to be. And perception is guided by expectation. If you've ever looked in the fridge for the barbecue sauce that's in a jar that you're quite certain is green, and you can't find it, it's often because the jar is really brown. It could be right in the front, with the words BARBECUE SAUCE staring you in the face, but since it's brown and you're looking for green, it may as well be invisible.

Babies are born with no idea of what things in their field of vision are most important. Their vision gives everything equal value. Little by little they learn what matters, and in doing so learn not to see things that seem not to matter as much.

So what's reality? We're looking for a scenario that allows for the fact that day after day no one on our block walks into the maple tree at the corner because all of us can see that it's there. You simply are not going to buy the idea that if you really, really, *really* don't believe that tree is there, you could walk right through where everyone else thinks it is, are you? That's because you are neither a quantum physicist nor a mystic. (If you said, "What tree?" then you're well on your way to one or the other.) But we also need a scenario that can encompass the idea that each of us creates our own reality according to the idiosyncrasies of the way our senses gather and transmit information to the brain, and how the brain's few billion synaptic pathways are constructed and connected in each individual person.

Let's try the everyone-stand-around-in-a-circle model that we used in the Ambiguity section. And we'll represent each person's sensory experience and data as a wedge-shaped field of vision. In the middle of the circle is an infinitely sided polygon (known as a circle) that represents generally agreed-upon reality. The maple tree at the end of the block is in there. Very close, in front of each individual, is a small area that is not

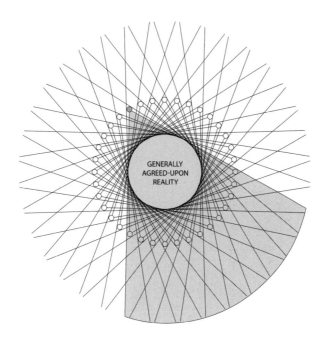

within the field of vision of the people on either side. That's a private reality where our secrets live. Those secrets might be within the field of vision of the people across from us, but they're probably too far away to notice. There's an area a bit in front of each individual that's shared only with the people nearby, on either side. That reality is shared by the members of our immediate family, our coworkers, or, for instance, everyone who thinks that the Cubs are jinxed. There's a very large area behind each person that that individual is totally ignorant of. That might be where other people's religions are.

So next time someone tells you he's a realist, ask him to explain exactly what he means. The further he takes that explanation, the more foolish it's likely to sound.

Orientation

The sun is not only the source of life-giving energy, but it has also had an effect on our language here and there as well. I often wonder about the birth order of word siblings like *knife, fork,* and *spoon,* for instance, and *north, east, south,* and *west.* It seems obvious, once we think about it, that people must have had concern about the appearance and the disappearance of the sun long before they cared about where those ice sheets were coming from or where penguins could be found. East would have preceded west, as attention was drawn to it in the morning. They wouldn't have started worrying about the sun disappearing until at least mid-afternoon.

So the sun determined the first directional dichotomy, and provided the framework for the second—north and south—and, hence, all those three-letter combinations you find in the south–southeast corner of crossword puzzles.

A Sanskrit word meaning "to arise" slowly evolved through Greek, Latin, and French to become *orient,* another word we now use to describe the Far East. Our nomadic ancestors would arise every morning needing to know right away in which direction to head out—the sun made getting oriented easy except, perhaps, on overcast days.

Building on that tradition, to face the Orient became "to orient" and

The English word *east* derives from the Old Teutonic word *austono,* which meant "from the east." The *aus* part of that word is related to the Latin word *aurora*—the dawn.

West also grew from a Teutonic word that originated in the Latin word *vesper*—the evening star, and therefore "evening." Ultimately *vesper* can be

(continued on next page)

traced to a Sanskrit word meaning "down," the direction the sun is heading as the evening star appears.

The origins of *north* are obscure, but there are possible links to ancient words meaning "left," which, of course, would be the case for a person facing east.

South is similarly uncertain, but may have originated in the prehistoric Germanic word *sunnon,* an etymology that suggests a meaning such as "region of the sun" or "side on which the sun appears." And this would be the point of view of someone facing east from their home in the northern hemisphere.

Source: John Ayto, *Dictionary of Word Origins,* Arcade Publishing, 1990.

that process became known as "orientation." Ultimately *orientation* lost its direct tie to the East and has come to mean learning our location. Now, everyone on earth starts the day in a different place, and so even if two people wanted to set out for the same destination, they'd have to embark in different directions. Thus we each have our different orientations. Since we each see the world from where we are, each individual's reality and orientation are intrinsically intertwined with those of our friends, coworkers, neighbors, and family members. There's a lot of overlap.

But one of the objectives of this book is to observe polarized opposites and to find a synthesis that can unite them. Specifically, the principles that ambigrams most readily represent are found in Eastern philosophy and Western science. Both set off from the same place—observing the universe around us—but then proceeded by separate paths: one by painstaking and rigorous experiment, the other by deep thought. The twain met long ago, but left the station in different directions.

Symmetry

For most people, symmetry is something they notice occasionally and take lightly. It almost always involves "mirror image" (horizontally bilateral) symmetry—two matching lamps on either side of a room, or maybe bookends. But, when William Blake wrote,

Tyger, tyger, burning bright
In the forests of the night,
What immortal hand or eye
Could frame thy fearful symmetry?

he was surely talking about something deeper than the similarity between the right and left sides of the tiger. Dictionary definitions of symmetry often mention correspondence of parts on either side of an axis only *after* the idea of pleasing proportion, beauty, and harmony—more likely the idea that Blake had in mind. The two definitions can be reconciled, as we have seen, by the idea that in symmetry, we find both truth and beauty.

For instance, the first definition of *symmetry* in *Webster's New Collegiate Dictionary,* 1961 edition, is: "due or balanced proportion; beauty of form arising from such harmony." The second definition, "correspondence in size, shape, and relative position, of parts that are on op-

Symmetry

THE BEAUTY OF AN
ENTIRETY, WHICH
ORIGINATES FROM
THE HARMONY OF
ITS COMPONENTS.

CORRESPONDING
POSITION, SHAPE,
& SIZE OF PARTS
ON THE OPPOSITE
SIDES OF AN AXIS.

posite sides of a dividing line or median plane," is more in keeping with its root component words, which mean "same" and "measure." At the beginning of the first definition is the notation *"now rare."* And the second definition differs from the way we use the word in common everyday speech, being a good bit broader in scope than the bookends example.

Among the ambigrams in this book, "Balance" and "Waterfalls" represent mirror-image symmetry, as do the Rorschach-style paintings and the "Transparent" and "Starship" sculptures. But most of the ambigrams in this book, including "Symmetry," in this section, are examples of rotational symmetry. Rather than looking the same when viewed in a mirror, they look the same when turned 180 degrees. While this may not be what we normally think of as symmetry, its symmetry *can* be demonstrated. In a two-step process, an image of rotational symmetry can be achieved by producing a vertical mirror image, and then a horizontal mirror image of that vertical mirror image.

Following the shadow to the bottom and right of each letter from one step to the next makes it easier to see these two stages. The two steps require first a horizontal axis and then a vertical axis. Although it's not quite as easy to see, a 45-degree angle could serve as a single axis for rotational symmetry.

Not all symmetries are configured around a single axis. Mineral crystals expand our ideas of symmetry beyond the bookends to include symmetries based on two axes, three axes, four axes, and more. Typography can do the same*: whereas this capital **A** is symmetrical on either side of a vertical axis, this **E** is identical above and below a horizontal axis, and this **X** is symmetrical on both a horizontal and a vertical axis. The diameter of a circle represents a central axis regardless of its angle and so, allotting one per degree, this circular **O** would have 180 axes. A sphere (a crystal ball, for instance) would boast even more.

The point is that there is a lot more symmetry around than we might think. In his book *Das Energi,* Paul Williams says it this way:

"Truth is what sounds right.

Beauty is what looks right.

means be aware."

BEWARE

of symmetry.

*The symmetries referred to are true for the letters used on this page, but may vary somewhat when other fonts are used.

Truth & Beauty

Where do our ideas of beauty originate? I believe they are determined by the physical laws of nature and, as humans evolved under the same conditions as the rest of Earth's animals, vegetables, and minerals, our aesthetic tastes are woven into the patterns of our DNA.

It's clear that the external human form is intended to be symmetrical about a vertical axis, or that it functions best in its environment when it is. Such is the case with just about all living things. Animals, vegetables, and minerals are all subject to the most basic laws of physics and, of those, the law of gravity is the most prevalent in everyday life. Things are symmetrical so they don't fall over.

Taking that thought a bit further, things that lack the capability of locomotion—trees, rocks, mountains, for instance—are heavier at the bottom than at the top. Were they top-heavy, they'd either fall down or roll over. Human attempts to re-create what God provided succeed where they best emulate the characteristics of natural phenomena. Pyramids not only resemble mountains, but they seem to have derived from that form the trait of longevity as well.

The proportions found in Greek and Roman architecture are considered classic, and are often referred to in discussions of aesthetics.

There's the Golden Rectangle—a mathematical ratio found in the proportions of many classical buildings and natural organisms as well. On a more down-to-earth level, an excellent analogy can be drawn between Roman columns and tree trunks. When you see inexpensive replacement columns on the porches of urban Victorian houses, the diameter at the top and bottom is often the same. It's much easier to manufacture them that way. But they look clumsy and oafish in comparison to what our eyes are used to seeing: the subtle and graceful tapering of a column that's narrower at the top than the bottom. Emulating the tree trunk, the column gets lighter as it visually lifts away from the ground, and thereby lightens the appearance of the entire structure. Two- and three-story columns virtually soar.

Ultimately, what nature displays is natural, of course, and in harmony with the laws of physics. Indeed, nature's creations are the laws of physics incarnate. Thus, they represent truth. At least since Aristotle said so about 300 years before the Christian era, art has been defined as an imitation of nature. And although many modern and postmodern artists have chosen to sidestep the idea of visual beauty as a measure of achievement, it may be that they have merely shifted their focus from visual beauty to intellectual or philosophical truth.

As K. C. Cole writes in *The Universe and the Teacup,* "the same properties that make a snowflake appealing underlie the laws that control the universe. Truth and beauty are two sides of a coin."

Asymmetry

My work reveals a strong affinity to symmetry, whether it be the visual and physical symmetry exemplified by the 180-degree rotations of most of my ambigrams or the mirror-image reflections of my Rorschach-style pieces, the conceptual symmetry of words and ideas like hot and cold, male and female, day and night, and other yin/yang relationships, or my proclivity toward the use of complementary colors: red/green, blue/orange, or my favorites, black and white.

Most simply stated, symmetry is what remains the same following a change of some sort. And it is that very situation that we call truth, whether in the science laboratory or the courtroom.

When we seek to understand what's real and true, we must look at a situation from a number of differing vantage points. Scientists must test a hypothesis under varied circumstances in order to gain confidence that the hypothesis will stand as an aspect of scientific truth. Juries need to hear from several witnesses, and when stories corroborate each other—that is, remain the same even from a different person's point of view—our juries usually believe that the consistent story is the truth.

But we can't quite say that everything is either symmetrical or asym-metrical. While nature is replete with innumerable examples of sym-

In design, perfect symmetry is considered static, and thus less interesting than asymmetry, or an almost perfect symmetry. Even if subtle, the departures from otherwise unwavering regularity are said to invigorate the design as a whole. I've pushed the subtlety aspect of that concept pretty far with the ambigrams in this book. Each is exactly and 100 percent perfectly symmetrical. And the rectangular chunks of wording that appear above and below them, while they are linguistically and informationally different, are intended to be as similar in appearance as I can possibly make them. The fact that they are made up of different words and letters is subtle indeed. Two nonvisual factors provide dissymmetry and prevent the ambigram from existing in a static equilibrium: most of the letters in an

(continued on page 54)

metry, few—if any—are perfectly symmetrical. In both scientific and artistic symmetries, an often overlooked phenomenon is the concept of "dissymmetry." Distinct from "asymmetry," dissymmetry is a state of *almost* perfect symmetry. One might look at the shape of a tree, or a leaf, obtaining at a glance the impression of symmetry. And while no one would expect the branches and leaves of a tree to be perfectly symmetrical, the apparent symmetries are critical to an understanding of those systems.

Trees, cats, mountains, and people's faces and bodies tend to be pretty symmetrical, and up to a point, the more symmetrical they are, the more attractive we find them. But imagine how much less appealing they'd all be if they were absolutely identical on both sides on an axis. Not that they'd be unattractive, exactly, but they'd look artificial— nature shies away from perfect symmetry, while manufacturing tends toward it. This is why Cindy Crawford's mole is so important. It's the tiny spot of asymmetry that assures us that she's a beautiful female human being, and not the artificial creation of a civilization from another galaxy, or the fashion industry.

Aesthetically, absolute symmetry seems static and lifeless. But symmetry is energized, enlivened, by a little bit of asymmetry. The "flaws" in the symmetry create a tension, an excitement, as the viewer is attracted simultaneously by the placid beauty of the dominant symmetry and the disruptive detail. When most of an image is essentially symmetrical, the asymmetrical parts may stand out, even if tiny.

Rorschach-style inkblot images have always fascinated viewers, as they unlock the imagination, and perhaps thereby unlock the unconscious realms of the mind. Knowing that the markings in an inkblot

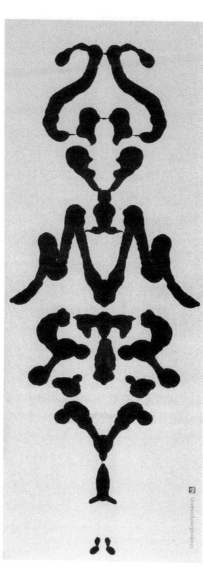

ambigram metamorphose into other letters when reversed; and each of those accompanying sentences provides a different idea of the word's meaning.

symmetry Asymmetry

image are random and unintentional, people generally regard them in a sort of "out of focus" way: if there's no intended image there, how could we expect all the details to be just right? We can picture the butterfly or the two dragons even when some parts may be missing or other extraneous shapes have been added on. Perhaps because the minute details can be overlooked, the overall blot is assumed to be perfectly symmetrical. In fact, however, it can be quite difficult to make an inkblot image that's perfectly symmetrical. In every inkblot print I've ever studied closely, there are small asymmetries, usually near the center, along the fold or spine of the image, where the pigment transfers imperfectly. We understand the idea of the perfectly symmetrical image. But when the anomalies are discovered, there's an exciting sense of discovery. Questions like "Why?" and "How?" leap to mind. It's so much easier to relate to something that's imperfect, like us, than something flawless.

A rule of thumb for experiencing these phenomena would be: if you stand back, you'll see the beauty. In close, you'll see the individual character.

So there's a dance of sorts going on—a tension-filled interaction between symmetry and asymmetry. Like yin and yang, they are a pair of obvious opposites, but what we see at work in our surroundings is the dissymmetry that is born of the interrelationship between these two extremes. The symmetry that exists between symmetry and asymmetry is the Tao.

Reflect

Viewing things from a different point of view may only mean looking in a different direction. Like back instead of forward. Today I caught myself looking back on an experience in which I had caught myself looking back.

I walked into the hotel bathroom, clicked on the light, and stood at the counter. No more than three feet away, I saw a familiar face. The recognition seemed to be mutual. "Of course," I thought, "it's only my own image in the glass." Everything seemed perfect . . . symmetrical. The hair color was right, the eyes were the same, even the teeth. When I moved my mouth the image moved its mouth. My eyebrow, its eyebrow. Not a moment later, either—in the same instant! Was the person in the mirror *thinking* the same thing? Was he wondering about me? I leaned a little to one side. In the mirror in front of me, I could see the mirror behind me across the room. In the mirror behind me, I saw the image of my image in the mirror in front of me. It was looking at the image across

Retrospect. Enamel, glass eye, mirror, wood frame, 1996.

Personal Reflections. Oil on canvas, 2004.

from it and appeared to be wondering whether it was thinking the same thoughts. But I couldn't make eye contact with it. It was concentrating on another familiar image across from it in the mirror in the mirror in the mirror. Reflections on reflections. Odd infinitum!

Mirrors should reflect a little before throwing back images.

Des Beaux-Arts, Jean Cocteau

TO TURN BACK ONE'S
THOUGHTS TO A PAR-
TICULAR SUBJECT; TO
MUSE OR MEDITATE.

reflect

TO TURN BACK, TO RE-
DIRECT MOTION IN THE
OPPOSITE DIRECTION;
TO ACT AS A MIRROR.

Balance

Balance is a good thing, right? Sounds perfect. In fact, it's probably a lot like perfection, in all the best and worst ways. If a person or a situation were to achieve perfect balance, there would only be one possible place to go from there: losing the balance. In time, the balance *will* be lost. Until the balance is lost, there is anxiety, waiting for that moment. The tightrope walker pauses, remains motionless. The audience holds its breath . . . If the tightrope walker weren't making his way from one end of the wire to the other—if he just stayed where he paused, motionless, minute after minute going by—would there be any point in watching? The audience gets bored, begins to drift away, one by one.

That scenario suggests another possibility: time is suspended. Probably the closest a person can come to making that happen occurs in the extremely deep meditative state that Buddhist monks are said to achieve, reportedly for days, weeks, perhaps months. An observer would experience those long passages of time, but the monk would probably not be aware of anything at all, including the passage of time. He would also experience none of the imbalances and responses to imbalance that we associate with life.

For a Buddhist monk that might be a great achievement, but it's cer-

Since an ambigram is a somewhat physical manifestation of a concept, and gravity governs the balancing of physical things, and since constantly turning things upside down is no way to balance them, the word BALANCE is best represented by a mirror-image ambigram.

tainly not what most of us would consider a desirable life. When we make decisions and adopt behaviors in order to improve the balance of our lives, we intend to keep moving ahead, like a tightrope walker. A tightrope walker carries a long stick that he constantly tips, in tiny increments, from one side to the other. That stick is like everything we carry along: work, leisure, family and friends, exercise, sleep. We constantly tip the stick a little more in one direction, then the other, trying to keep ourselves from falling off. We're not trying to stay in one perfect place; we're trying to keep moving on the wire.

No sane person consciously strives for "perfection." Sane people know that it's not achievable. But who does not attempt to improve every day to avoid repeating past mistakes? When those attempts are not a part of a person's life, then that life is off track and the person is unbalanced, either as the result of some misfortune, or surely heading toward one.

Balance is an excellent thing to strive for, but maybe not to attain. It's the striving that's good, because it's the striving that's life. It helps to have a carrot at the end of the stick.

Polarized

> At the very roots of Chinese thinking and feeling there lies the principle of polarity, which is not to be confused with the ideas of opposition or conflict. In the metaphors of other cultures, light is at war with darkness, life with death, good with evil, and the positive with the negative, and thus an idealism to cultivate the former and be rid of the latter flourishes throughout much of the world. To the traditional way of Chinese thinking, this is as incomprehensible as an electric current without both positive and negative poles, for polarity is the principle that + and −, north and south, are different aspects of the same system, and that the disappearance of either one of them would be the disappearance of the system.
>
> *Tao: The Watercourse Way,* Alan Watts

Taoism avoids value judgments. Yang is not better than yin any more than south is better than north. They're relative. And relatives. On the other hand, we're quite sure that good is better than bad. Yet this can be true only in a way made possible by defining something comparatively in terms of itself. *Good* and *bad* have to be thought of as relative terms in order to have any real meaning for us. Taken as absolutes, we could hardly apply them to anything that happens in our lives. Every silver lining has a cloud, and vice versa.

Sometimes words take on value judgments. In the sciences, polarization is simply an observable phenomenon, but socially we tend to think of polarization in negative terms. "When my spouse and I argue, we just get polarized," we admit to our shrinks, our friends, or ourselves. Some of us pay a hundred or so dollars an hour to worry about something that can as easily be considered good as bad!

Picture a couple standing on a seesaw, near the middle. Their balance is uncertain, as all relationships are, but they are touching. As something comes between them, they back away from each other slowly, deliberately, matching step for step until they are standing at the ends, behind the handlebars. (After many years of relating, couples often develop the ability to leap back in astonishingly precise synchronization, reaching the ends in one or two leaps.) But the danger in such situations is most present when one person steps off, falls off, or is propelled off the seesaw. As long as they can stay on, even if polarized, they can find their way back to each other. The couple is still balanced and, sometimes slowly, sometimes precipitously, they can return to their former positions at the middle. The balance may be threatened when the couple moves away from the middle, but the ability to polarize may protect each individual, and ensure the continuation of the relationship.

polarized

HAVING MOVED TO
POSITIONS OF THE
GREATEST POSSI-
BLE DIVERGENCE.

Magnetic

I feel drawn to this word, as if pulled by a force so great I am not able even to comprehend it. I cannot resist its attraction. And yet I feel as though I have a choice. How to approach it? From the south, as I normally approach all words?

But wait. The attraction must be mutual. This word was drawn *by* me as well. But the attraction must not be based on the alignment of electrons, for no matter what vantage point I adopt, the same end of me is attracted to the word. Apparently it doesn't matter from which direction I approach it. Opposites attract, and I am not opposed to this word. Obviously we are unlike each other. Likes don't like each other, and I like it.

If opposites attract, how can they stay opposed? If opposed to each other, can they consummate their attraction? I've lost my way in the word woods without a linguistic lodestone. I've fallen into a verbal vortex. If allowed, could it become a spoken spiral? It must be time to stop turning the book in favor of turning the page.

A FORCE OF ATTRACTION EXISTING BETWEEN OPPO- SITE POLES & REPULSION BETWEEN LIKE POLES. (IT WORKS WITH PEOPLE, TOO.)

maGnetic

A STATE OF CONSTANT DIPOLA- RITY; A NORTH POLE CANNOT BE ISOLATED FROM A SOUTH POLE ANY MORE THAN YANG CAN BE ISOLATED FROM YIN.

Electricity

Magnetism and electricity are the yin and yang of electromagnetism. Both are based on polarized electric charges, positive and negative, that elementary particles of matter possess. Like charges repel each other while unlike charges attract. Originally the word *electricity* referred to what we now know as static electricity—the force that makes two objects attract each other when friction between them causes charged electrons to hop from object one to object two. But that's still a little hard to comprehend.

Sticking your finger in an open socket is the only way to really understand electricity. It feels as if your arm were pure energy and no longer a part of your body. Soon (something like one one-thousandth of a second later), some part of your mind understands that it wouldn't be too much longer until *none* of you was part of your body, and you would cease to exist. Thus enlightened, you remove your finger from the socket.

Legend has it that Benjamin Franklin, not having any empty sockets handy, sought enlightenment with a kite, a key, and a jar. The "discovery" of electricity came to him in a flash. Even though we currently generate our own electricity, it's still probably fair to think of it as trapped lightning. Take note that on page 67 is one of the rare instances of lightning striking twice in the same place.

THE CURRENT YIN AND YANG
OF ELECTRICITY ARE THE DI-
RECT AND ALTERNATING VA-
RIETIES. DC'S CIRCUIT MOVES
IN ONLY 1 DIRECTION, WHILE
AC'S REVERSES FREQUENTLY.

A STATE OF ENERGY EXISTING
IN ALL ATOMS THAT IS CREA-
TED BY THE ATTRACTION BE-
TWEEN THE POSITIVE CHARGE
OF A PROTON AND THE NEGA-
TIVE CHARGE OF AN ELECTRON

Gravity

This is no time for levity. This is a grave subject (as are we all). It's time to get down to some serious etymology. We must dig down to the roots.

The word *gravity* refers specifically to the attraction between the Earth and any other hunk of matter. Since we and our languages developed here on Earth, we see the heavens as being "up." So whereas relationships between things in space may seem more lateral, we are definitely *down* here, and anything coming toward us from the sky is definitely coming down—that's gravity.

The root of *gravity* in modern English is the word *grave.* The two most common usages of the word *grave* are: 1. "a place of burial," and 2. "having weight or importance." In the first case, the word *grave* evolved from the Old English *grafen,* meaning to dig. In the second instance it came from the Latin *gravis,* which meant heavy or important. A downward direction is central to both meanings.

In any case, if it weren't for gravity we wouldn't know which way is up. Without gravity to pull things "down," there would be no such concept as up *or* down. This is an excellent example of the yin/yang principle that nothing exists except in relation to its opposite.

In conclusion, I'll be brief. The absence or opposite of gravity is weightlessness. Therefore, gravity is the soul of wt.

IS THE
SOUL
OF WT.

gravity

IS THE FORCE WITH
WHICH ONE ENTITY
ATTRACTS ANOTHER

Up/Dn

The popular phrase this ambigram demonstrates captures the spirit of Newton's third law of motion—for every action there is an equal and opposite reaction—and the essence of yin and yang as well. It is most readily demonstrated by the force of gravity. Even the most towering home runs and foul balls eventually make it back to Earth. But the idea can appropriately be extended to the fame of celebrities, hemlines, personal moods, and a myriad of situations beyond the jurisdiction of the laws of physics.

It's tough to escape the music of yin and yang. Even the seemingly capricious vicissitudes of individual minds and societal trends dance to that tune. It could very well be that the laws of physics are encoded in the strands of everyone's DNA, or that throughout our emergence from the world of physics into the realm of biology, and our continued presence within both, we have assimilated those principles into our individual and collective subconsciouses and hence, behavior. Fact is, we need balance.

What drives this tendency is obviously more than gravity. Our decisions are based on our perceptions of our surroundings. While "what" is going up, since nothing can happen in isolation, conditions are changing, often as a result of "its" ascent. Sometimes it seems like the stock market might work this way.

WHAT
GOES
up
MUST
COME

As the Dow Jones average rises, people feel good about investing. They perceive the positive momentum of the Dow, are encouraged that it will continue to rise, and so they buy. As a result the Dow does continue to rise and stocks increase in value. This continues until the average is so high that investors, evaluating that condition, begin to question the strength of the momentum. Buying slows, selling begins. A new condition takes effect, and responding to it, investors sell and the Dow falls.

This ebb and flow of the stock market (which could be referred to as "Dowism" but for some reason isn't) is parallel to the human emotions that respond to the law of gravity. A hot-air balloon ride (I'm told) is exciting as it begins and exhilarating as the balloon soars over the countryside. But if the balloon were to rise beyond its passengers' expectations, nervousness would set in. That might have to do with unintentional lateral motion at first, if indeed there were any, but whether the balloon were directly over its point of origin or a hundred miles out to sea, its being subject to the law of gravity would eventually be the primary concern of the unfortunate occupants. It is this very concern that has thus far kept me out of hot-air balloons, and nervous on airplanes. "Look not thou down but up!" wrote Robert Browning. I couldn't agree more with this advice, and I try to follow it. When I'm on the ground, looking up affords the pleasures of enjoying the sky. When people are up in an aircraft they seem mostly to look down—longingly, it seems to me.

Waterfalls

Water intrigues us. We love to go to the ocean, swim in pools, take showers, relax in baths and Jacuzzis. We can be transfixed by water moving from one place to another and so we picnic by the river and play, as children, in streams. But of all the forms of water that attract us, no other has the compelling power of waterfalls. Why? Simply because water falls. We usually take the effects of gravity for granted. Most things simply aren't in a constant state of falling. But waterfalls, in common experience, *never* stop. Each one is a part of a never-ending cycle and thus a direct experience of something that's virtually infinite, and available to all of us. As such, in a most awe-inspiring manner, waterfalls appeal to our subconscious appreciation for both the force of gravity and the many cycles inherent in life. Little wonder then that the Taoists consistently refer to water as demonstrating the principles of the Tao.

Water is always yielding. It takes the path of least resistance. It seeks not the highest place, but the lowest. Avoiding confrontation, it goes around whatever gets in its way. Yet it wears down everything in its path. Water gets its way by yielding, a principle that is frequently referred to in the Asian martial arts.

The Tao is also about returning, and water demonstrates this principle as well: evaporating in millions of gallons a day from the ocean, descending to earth as rain and snow, then beginning its long meandering trip, returning to the sea. A journey of a thousand miles begins with a single drop.

WATERFALLS

It was hard to imagine an upside-down waterfall, so this one is a mirror-image ambigram.

Minimum

Lao-tzu, the sixth-century B.C. philosopher who is regarded as the father of Taoism, wrote, "The Tao does nothing, and yet nothing is left undone." This important passage addresses the fundamental Taoist concept of non-action. But since we are incapable of total non-action—even in the deepest meditation our internal organs are performing their functions at some minimal level: we are breathing, pulsating, digesting, and so forth—scholars have often interpreted this passage as "doing the minimum."

The concept of resistance is at odds with the Taoist approach to life. Choosing the path of *least* resistance is more in keeping with Taoist philosophy, and once again, water shows us the way. To go with the flow is to get from point A to point B with a minimum of effort. Accepting itself as being subject to the law of gravity, water travels accordingly, circumnavigating its obstacles and eroding them in the process. Water does nothing of its own accord, and yet everything is affected by water. By doing nothing more than going along with the law of gravity, water shapes and nourishes the entire planet.

As the "minimum" ambigram on the facing page demonstrates by giving almost no clues as to what letters are there, doing the minimum is *minimum*

often sufficient. It is a happy coincidence, of course, that the word *minimum* requires so little, because in *every* ambigram I have tried to do the minimum: to perform only the manipulations necessary to provide both readability and reversibility. Decisions are made on the basis of what is required to meet these ends. Nothing is added that will not aid in the achievement of these goals. Form follows function.

It is certainly true that I have tried to draw the letterforms in a beautiful fashion, but that beauty is directly related to readability. The letterforms of most Western languages were brought to their classic form by the Romans, who instilled in them all the beauty of shape and proportion that were manifested in their architecture. It was their architecture, in fact, for which classic Roman capital letters were developed. Though the alphabet has undergone a myriad of stylistic experiments in the past two millennia, most of the letters we read throughout our lives are primarily based on that classic Roman form. The flow of readability is best enhanced by providing the reader's eye with attractive and familiar letterforms. In a manner of speaking, doing the minimum brings us back to the basics.

The "GoWithTheFlow" ambigram follows the "doing the minimum" model by using no more decoration than necessary—it's just that a lot was necessary for the complexity of this four-word ambigram. The

Gothic "blackletter" style is naturally more decorative than letters based on the Roman forms, and while less familiar, it is, nevertheless, reasonably familiar to Western European and American readers. Its decorative aspects help disguise some of the more excessive letter distortions that the ambigram required. The bouncy baseline is necessary to distinguish the individual words, and while that bounciness is very much out of place with blackletter tradition, I like it because it creates a bit of a fluid flow. On the other hand, the blackletter style is pure irony, given the strict discipline that is implied by the military regularity of the dominant vertical strokes, and the rigidity that we associate with the character of groups that have used it the most over the years: the Germanic people—the Nazis, in particular—and various Christian churches.

Wavelength

As waterfalls represent water in continuous motion, waves are water in continual motion. Not content simply to watch these compelling phenomena, human beings have tried to become directly involved and have devised various craft with which to ride them—to go with the flow. As it turns out, waves are much more suitable for sports than waterfalls are.

Surfers, besides attempting to perfect their athletic skills, spend hours learning to understand every nuance of the waves they ride. One of the more predictable aspects of waves is their frequency. Their rhythmic repetitions are familiar to everyone who has ever set foot on the beach, and to physicists, whether they've ever waxed a surfboard or not.

The word *waves* may evoke the image of a beautiful day at the beach, but water is perhaps only the most visible and tangible of the many things that come to us in waves. When energy is transferred through physical matter, a disturbance is created, and the material responds (in an equal and opposite manner) to restore its state of equilibrium. The pattern created by the stimulus and the response is wave motion. This motion takes place without any corresponding progressive movement. The individual parts of the material, as the energy disturbance passes, come to rest in their original position. Were this not the case, a Los An-

Commissioned by Brian Hupf, Massachusetts.

(IT WORKS EITHER WAY)

Wavelength

IN A SERIES OF WAVES,
THE DISTANCE (IN UNITS
OF TIME OR SPACE) FROM
TROUGH TO TROUGH OR
FROM CREST TO CREST

geles baseball fan, returning from a Dodger Stadium food stand, might find his empty seat and his friends three sections to the left of where he left them. Fortunately, waves don't work that way.

In visual terms, the wave pattern suggests various relationships between yin and yang and other graphic representations of physical principles. Below is a diagram of waves.

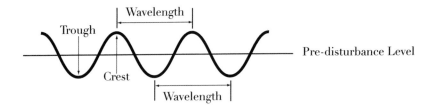

A single wave, pictured from trough to trough, resembles the curve of normal distribution.

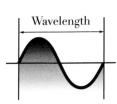

A single wavelength measured not from trough to trough or crest to crest, but from a point where the wave pattern crosses the pre-disturbance level to the next instance of that intersection, reproduces the line that separates yin and yang.

An extended coil spring toy can be "whipped" to demonstrate the action of waves, and when stretched and viewed laterally, the toy itself bears a close resemblance to a series of waves.

Graphing the oscillation of a pendulum results in the same sine curve as the oscillation of particles in a wave. Simultaneous representation of two sine curves in phase opposition suggests the double helix of DNA.

Isolating a single wavelength from the two sine curves in phase opposition yields a reasonable facsimile of the graphic infinity symbol, while a three-dimensional model of that symbol is a looped wave pattern two wavelengths in circumference.

Musing on these analogies can be intriguing, but I've got other concerns at the moment: the wave is coming around again, and this time I don't want to spill my beer.

Normal Distribution

I was tense as our plane left the runway. The trajectory was, as usual, a gradual angle at first, then more dramatic as it climbed toward cruising altitude. As the plane approached thirty-six thousand feet, its thrust and angle moderated, and my tension did the same. After a while, from the vantage point of my window seat, I watched as scattered hills rose and fell, increased in number, grew to mountains, and tapered off again, ultimately disappearing into the plains. Little streams joined to form bigger ones; small rivers followed suit, eventually conspiring to create the Mississippi. Later, the process was reversed. Next to me, on the aisle, my wife caught some of the scenery. Most of the passengers missed the views as they sat in the five seats in the middle of each row down the middle of the plane. There were, as usual, among the three hundred or so passengers, a few old people, and some middle-aged folks, a large number of young adults, several teenagers, and a few children. Just about everyone got up once or twice during the course of the five-hour flight. A few, mostly in the middle seats, stayed put throughout. A handful, mostly children, spent much of the time roaming the aisles, and the attendants were on their feet for all but the few minutes at either end of the flight. They were busiest around the halfway point as they saw to the distribution of lunch. As calm as I get on an airplane,

A NATURAL PATTERN
REPRESENTING DATA
GATHERED FROM A
RANDOM SAMPLING
OF A GIVEN GROUP.

NORMALDISTRIBUTION

HUMAN BEHAVIOR, &c:
IN NATURE, THE ENDS
JUSTIFY THE MEANS,
SO HUMANS AMOUNT
TO A HILL OF BEIN'S.

As if to prove the normality of the curve of normal distribution, nature provides us with some wonderful examples, most often due to the natural distribution of the forces of erosion. The normal effects of wind and water are displayed throughout the landscape, occasionally creating archetypal "normal" hills.

I read, slept, and, after a brief period of turbulence, read again as we crossed the middle of the country.

As we neared our destination the pilot began the descent, a harbinger of the return of my anxiety. I tried to fend it off by looking out the window and concentrating on the scenery. I saw farmhouses scattered over the countryside and here and there, a small town. One or two tiny cars ran along the two-lane country roads. Little by little the farms grew smaller, the towns larger, and both grew closer together. Near the horizon the suburbs began. As we flew over, I could see that most of the houses were small one- and two-story homes. As the city came into sight, they were larger. Soon larger industrial buildings and an occasional small office building appeared. The cars looked bigger now, and there were more of them. Passing over the center of the city, I saw it rise to its fullest height where the population reached its greatest density.

With the landing gear down and the flight attendants buckled in, we began our final approach. Despite my concentration on patterns, my anxiety increased until we had landed. The awesome power required to lift a huge airplane into flight was demonstrated again, symmetrically, with the roar of the jets and the intense braking required to slow it down.

As I was leaving the plane, still in a state of hyperawareness from my adrenaline rush at landing, I noticed that the carpet of the gangway was quite worn down the center, less on either side, and was in virtually pristine condition next to the walls.

Reflecting on the experience, I mused that there are probably precious few flights with no turbulence at all, and very few that are terrifying ordeals. It had been an average flight. But as my legs relearned earthbound equilibrium, it felt good to be in my own time zone again. Back to normal.

The airport's gangway carpet and the stone step in this photo demonstrate that people can be just as effective as wind and water. Like any great truth, the curve of normal distribution works just as well upside down as it does right side up.

Time

When I looked for yin and yang within the concept of time, my first thought was "Wait. Time exists not in a duality, but in a triad of past, present, and future." But that's merely a trio of linguistic terms. It then dawned on me that the present is not my lifetime, this year or even this week. From an awareness point of view, what happened one minute ago has more in common with what happened ten thousand years ago than it does with what might happen one minute from now. Since I now know what happened one second ago, it is clearly in the category of the past, and since, conversely, there's no telling what will happen a second from now, that moment exists in the future. The present is, therefore, no more than the meeting point between the past and the future—no more a distinct entity than the line where yin meets yang. Both the past and the future are infinitely long and receding lines. The present is that indefinable point where they meet.

Yet the present is where we live. The past is history, and the future is conjecture. The present is life. Looking at it from a different point of view, the past and the future exist only as concepts in our minds, and the present, fleeting as it is, is reality.

· · ·

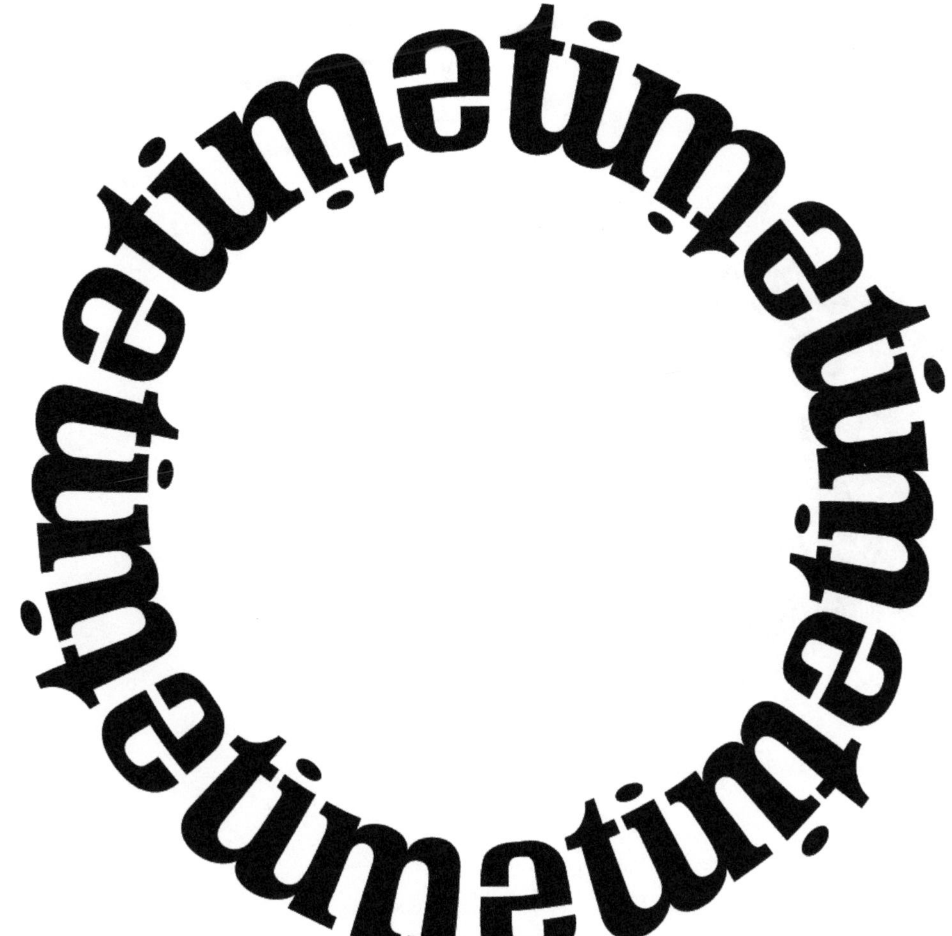
timetimetimetimetimetime

Let's look at the past, present, and future by means of a parable:

The two sides of a knife are irrelevant to the function of the knife. The edge where they meet is where the knife's essence, its raison d'être, exists. The finer, the less measurable that edge is (the less it even exists at all?), the sharper the blade, and the more effective the knife.

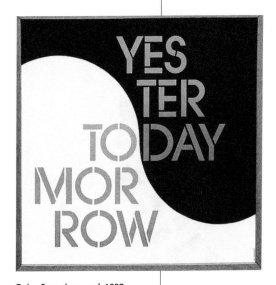

Today. Enamel on panel, 1987.

THE PRESENT IS REALITY.
THE PAST AND THE FUTURE
EXIST ONLY IN OUR MINDS.

THE PRESENT IS MERELY
A DIVIDING LINE BETWEEN
THE PAST AND THE FUTURE.

Past/Present/Future

The present lasts as long as the blink of an eye. The past and the future, on the other hand, are always around and will probably last forever. The past seems to keep getting bigger with more and more of our personal and cultural histories piling up in it. The future may be getting smaller, but how would we know? Certainly the future of anything we know is diminishing, but there may be an adequate supply of future for those whose lives remain beyond the limits of our imagination.

The ambigrams on these pages are intended to represent the endless conveyor belt of time, and the individual words are the experiences, the "life-bites" of our existence, the lines on the highway we're driving down.

Time can be thought of in purely visual terms, with the instantaneous present as the image that is currently being received on the retina. That idea seems to work in almost any situation. But let's get back in the car to extend the analogy to include the past and the future.

The future is what lies ahead along the road. The immediate and most predictable future is what's visible at any given moment. It will almost undoubtedly become part of our driving experience within a few seconds. What lies down the road beyond our scope is the more remote future. The farther away it is, the less predictable it becomes. The past, in much the same way, is what's in our rearview mirror, receding into the distance.

To fully enjoy the "past" and "future" ambigrams, don't turn this book like a steering wheel. The rearview-mirror approach will prove more successful for the bilateral nature of these ambigrams. I hope you're not reading this while you're driving, though. Any mirror will do.

Sometimes/Never

It may not be now.
It may not be soon.
It may be in the days-yet-to-come time.
But whether it's soon
or a long time from now,
there's a chance that it could happen sometime.

So never say "never"
and never say "always"—
there's always at least one exception.

And so if you ever
should hear in the hallways
a "never," it's always deception.

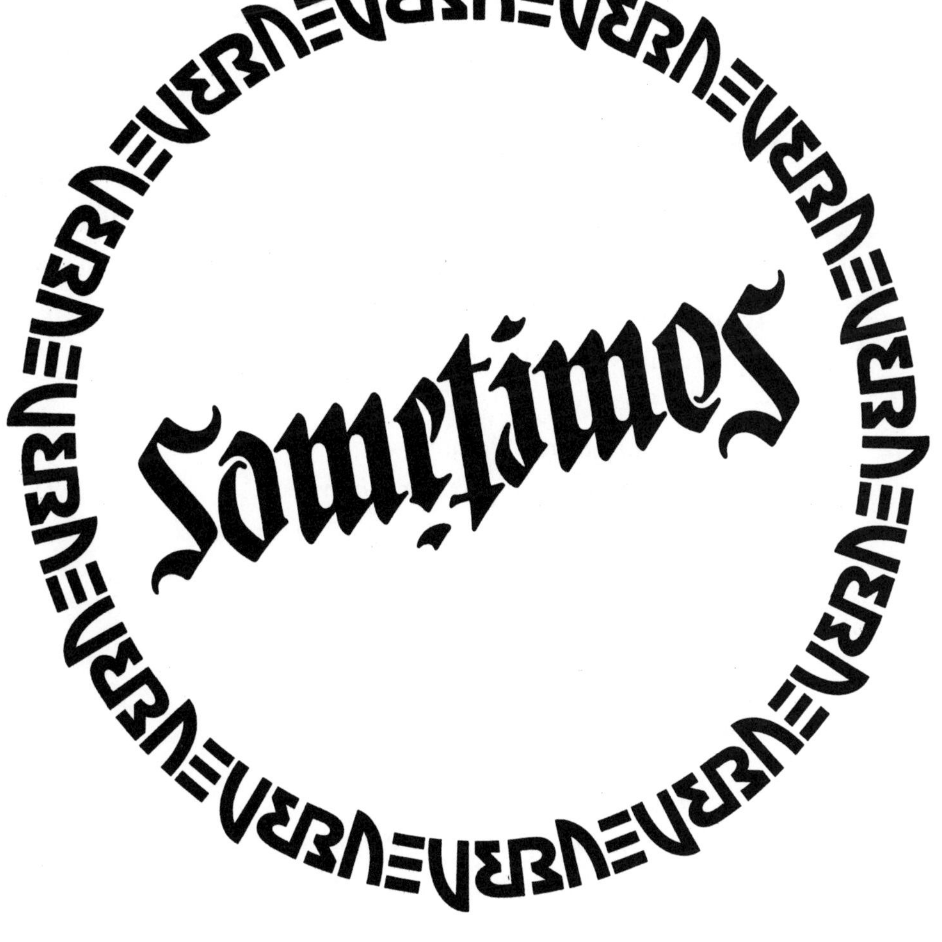
Sometimes
NEVER

Seasons

The popular song "Turn! Turn! Turn!" recorded by the Byrds in the late sixties was adapted by Pete Seeger from the Book of Ecclesiastes, which demonstrates the timelessness of the instinctive desire for balance. Citing a yin-and-yang relationship in each line, it seems quite Taoist in spirit: there are no value judgments—merely appropriate times for all things.

To every thing there is a season,
and a time to every purpose under heaven.
A time to be born, a time to die; a time to plant, and a time to reap;
A time to kill, a time to heal; a time to laugh, a time to weep.

To every thing there is a season,
and a time to every purpose under heaven.
A time to build up, a time to break down; a time to dance,
   and a time to mourn;
A time to cast away stones, a time to gather stones together.

To every thing there is a season,
and a time to every purpose under heaven.
A time of love, a time of hate; a time of war, a time of peace;
A time you may embrace, a time to refrain from embracing.

To every thing there is a season,
and a time to every purpose under heaven.
A time to gain, a time to lose; a time to rend, a time to sew;
A time to love, and a time to hate; a time of peace,
    I swear it's not too late.

Choice/Decide

The process of growth from infancy to adulthood, from dependence to independence, is so gradual that we are often not aware of the changes that take place until well after they have happened. Through most of that time we are told that we have to do certain things: "You have to go to school," "You have to go to bed now." Most people seem to spend the rest of their lives thinking that they "have to" do the things that they do: "I have to go to work," "I have to go to the dentist," "I have to pick up the kids."

Initially, it may seem like mere rhetoric, but *You don't have to do anything.* Next time you find yourself on the verge of saying "I have to . . . ," try replacing it by "I choose to . . . ," "I want to . . . ," "I've decided to . . . ," or "I'm going to . . . " It's incredibly liberating! When you say "I have to," you're inclined to believe it. The number of things that we "have to" do could easily have us feeling like slaves. Think of the frustration and damage to self-esteem that must come from thinking that you have to do everything that you do. And think of how much more powerful you'll feel when you say, "I've decided to."

At some indistinct point in our childhood, probably earlier than we can remember, we started doing things by choice but didn't realize it. Sometimes we decided to eat our baby food because that seemed to please Mom (undoubtedly a subconscious decision). We decided to eat our vegetables so we could have dessert (more likely a conscious decision). And then one day, we *decided* to defy our parents. We realized that we didn't *have* to finish our vegetables. They could sit there on the plate for all eternity. We also learned that our decisions had consequences.

As teenagers we learn freedom. Little by little, we discover that we are independent of our parents. Often we discover it by doing what we're not "supposed" to do. How could you discover your freedom if you never exercised it? As adults, however, we often forget what we learned. Our society seems to believe that there's something wrong with teenagers and that they'll be all right when they "grow up." And when we "grow up" we go back to doing things that we "have to."

Why do we "have to"? "Because if we don't, then . . ." That's right. There are consequences to be faced "if we don't." But there are also consequences if we do. We tend to use the word *consequence* only in a negative sense. But the word simply means "that which follows." When we *decide* to do what we "have to" do, there are consequences—usually consequences we want: we keep our jobs, we get raises, we have food to eat and a roof over our heads. Every time we do something, it's because we *decided* that the consequences of doing it would be more to our liking than the consequences of not doing it. Viewed that way, life is a pattern of decisions.

When we tell ourselves we have to do something, it's usually a situation where the choice between consequences is so obvious that conscious thought is not required. But that does not mean that we *have* to do it. "Have to" means that you have no choice. And you *always* have a

choice. There's a story about Jack Benny, avowed tightwad, in which he was accosted by a holdup man. "Your money or your life!" the crook demanded. When Jack didn't respond, the man grew impatient: "Hurry up, willya?" Benny replied, "I'm thinking, I'm thinking!"

Reminding yourself that you do things by choice gives you the sense that you are in control of your life. You realize that you have had a choice all along. You are where you are because of choices that you have made. You didn't *have* to go to Vietnam. You could have applied for conscientious objector status. You could have gone to Canada or to jail. Or crossed your fingers and hoped that you'd get a high number in the lottery (even not making a decision is a decision). You chose the option you were the most comfortable with. You are responsible for your own life.

Having a choice is the same as having freedom. Many people *choose* to not exercise their freedom. They forget that they have choices. Maybe they never consciously realized it.

The idea of consequences, "those things that follow," presumes that there is a sequence of events. Some events precede, others follow. Time, then, is a major factor in the freedom of choice.

If you *always* have a choice, at any given moment in time you have a decision to make. Fortunately, most of our actions fall into the category of "the choice is so obvious that I don't have to think about it." Seldom while we're walking downstairs do we decide to keep walking downstairs. Nevertheless, some hidden recess of our subconscious is deciding to keep walking down the stairs. Occasionally, of course, we decide to turn around and go back up.

Since time and events keep moving, as we've often heard, not making a decision is making a decision. Opting for the status quo (originally Latin terminology meaning "standing where" [you are]) is choosing to stand still and allow time and events to flow around us. Since trying to stand still while the water flows around and past us takes real effort, and that effort is never completely successful, to at least some degree we are "going with the flow." We should recognize that going with the flow reflects a decision—and much of the time, a sensible one. It is also usually the easiest decision we can make. For better or worse, our lives, and history at large, are governed for the most part by momentum. That's why it's so hard to change ourselves and our lives and our societies.

If we are making decisions at every moment of our lives, life is therefore a pervasive pattern of choices and decisions. Each decision brings new choices. We are always free to choose and, paradoxically, we are never free of the need to choose. If we were able to free ourselves from the obligation of choosing, we would surrender our choice to our surroundings and give up our freedom of control.

Every room has several doors,
several eithers, several ors.
Every door has several outcomes.
Some are sure,
with others, doubt comes.

When we make a decision, we can seldom be absolutely certain of what the consequences will be. Thus life is a constant exercise in insecurity. This is probably the reason why most people are happier feeling that they have to do things rather than being conscious of the fact that they are choosing their actions. They may complain about their jobs and their spouses, but they feel secure in those relationships. Are freedom and security mutually exclusive, a major yin and yang in life? Many times we hear of the trade-off between freedom and security, particularly as it pertains to civil rights. But how secure can we feel giving up control over our lives, not knowing what other events and other people's decisions are to come and what effect they might have?

Perhaps that, too, is cause for insecurity. But if we maintain the awareness that we are *choosing* momentum, *choosing* to go with the flow, with the knowledge that we can, at any time, change our minds and get out of the flow, or swim upstream, we can remain very secure. Security comes with the awareness that one has a choice.

Inertia

For thousands of years it was assumed that rest was the natural state of matter. Apparently overlooking friction, among other things, Aristotle and others seem to have thought that moving objects would eventually run out of steam and return to their "natural" behavior—resting.

Isaac Newton's first law of motion upset that apple cart: "Every body continues in its state of rest, or of uniform motion in a right line, unless it is compelled to change that state by forces impressed upon it." The name given to this phenomenon is *inertia*. Inertia therefore, it could be said, is the characteristic of matter that says nothing happens to it unless something happens to it. The entire notion of inertia may seem itself inert, but there's good reason that this ringing endorsement of the status quo should be Newton's first law. Its logic was basic enough that for a few hundred years his subsequent laws and theories, and those of others as well, were virtually unquestionable.

Then Einstein's relativity theory challenged Newton's laws. We now know that everything in the universe is in motion, outward bound from the Big Bang. Things at rest are at rest only relative to other things, which are probably resting nearby. It's like falling asleep on a train: you may be at rest, but it's still not all that restful. A geosynchronous satel-

*THE CHARACTERISTIC
OF MATTER WHEREBY
AN ENTITY IN MOTION
CONTINUES TO MOVE
UNLESS ACTED UPON
BY AN OUTSIDE FORCE.*

INERTIA

**THE CHARACTERISTIC
OF MATTER WHEREBY
A STATIONARY ENTITY
REMAINS STATIONARY
UNLESS ACTED UPON
BY AN OUTSIDE FORCE.**

lite, on the other hand, would appear to be at rest to the geo standing under it, but all the while it's whizzing through space at hundreds of miles per hour. Like everything else, motion is relative—it depends on your point of view.

Momentum

"Today is the first day of the rest of your life." This statement implies that we have choices and are in control of our destinies. While this is certainly true, it overlooks the power of momentum. We are the sum total of our hereditary and environmental pasts. With the possible exceptions of God and the Big Bang, nothing has ever started from nowhere. Everything owes its existence to something else. A number of something elses all interacting with each other. Everything has momentum.

The present may be the doorway to the future, but everything coming through that door comes from the past. Today most people live in the same place, relate to the same people, speak the same language, and operate from the same set of norms, values, and standards that they did yesterday. You can steer a car in any of a great number of directions, but the change in direction is both limited and gradual. Each change in degree is based on and is in relation to the previous degree. This need not be discouraging, however. After all, it is much easier to turn the wheels of a moving car than a parked one.

Early in the history of literary criticism, Socrates said that a story should have a beginning, a middle, and an end. This is the opposite of a "slice of life" approach in which a mere segment is treated, possibly leaving the reader wondering what may have preceded and what might have followed. This wondering is undoubtedly a result of the understanding that nothing exists in isolation—everything takes place in an infinite web of cause and effect.

Providing politicians, social activists, and medical ethicists with much to debate, science has shown that even the beginning and end of the life of a human being cannot be pinned down precisely. A fetus is preceded by a blastocyst, a single layer of cells arranged around an empty cavity, and the blastocyst in turn is preceded by the single-celled zygote. The zygote was preceded by and made from the union of a sperm and an egg, which in turn were produced by preceding human beings. At death, if there is a soul, it continues on in some way, and the body begins a new process toward some other form of energy.

In human behavior some might say that the ends justify the means, but this is a short-sighted vision. There are no ends. Each result is merely a factor in some other process. Everything exists in a state of momentum.

THE QUANTITY OF MOVEMENT

momentum

EQUALS MASS
TIMES VELOCITY.

Chain Reaction

For want of a nail, the shoe was lost;
for want of a shoe, the horse was lost;
for want of a horse, the soldier was lost;
for want of a soldier, the battle was lost;
for want of the victory, the kingdom was lost.

Since no event takes place in isolation, there are no ends but only means. Each and every occurrence is merely a link in an infinite chain. Perhaps the blacksmith, while he was shoeing the soldier's horse, was distracted by a gastrointestinal problem caused by something he had eaten the night before and therefore simply did a shoddy job.

At any given moment, there are an infinite number of identifiable chains of events operating simultaneously. Surely any hypercompulsive, omniscient scientist with infinite patience and a super-duper computer could trace any series backward in time, ultimately reaching back to the Big Bang. While the Big Bang itself was probably caused by another series of events, *that* idea is currently beyond our knowledge.

In addition, each chain is intersected by other chains. Not only is no single event isolated from all others, but no single chain of events can course through time unaffected by other chains.

Naturally, the loss of the battle had its effect on all subsequent history, including the apparently insignificant fact that you are currently reading this book. But then the want of a nail seemed insignificant too.

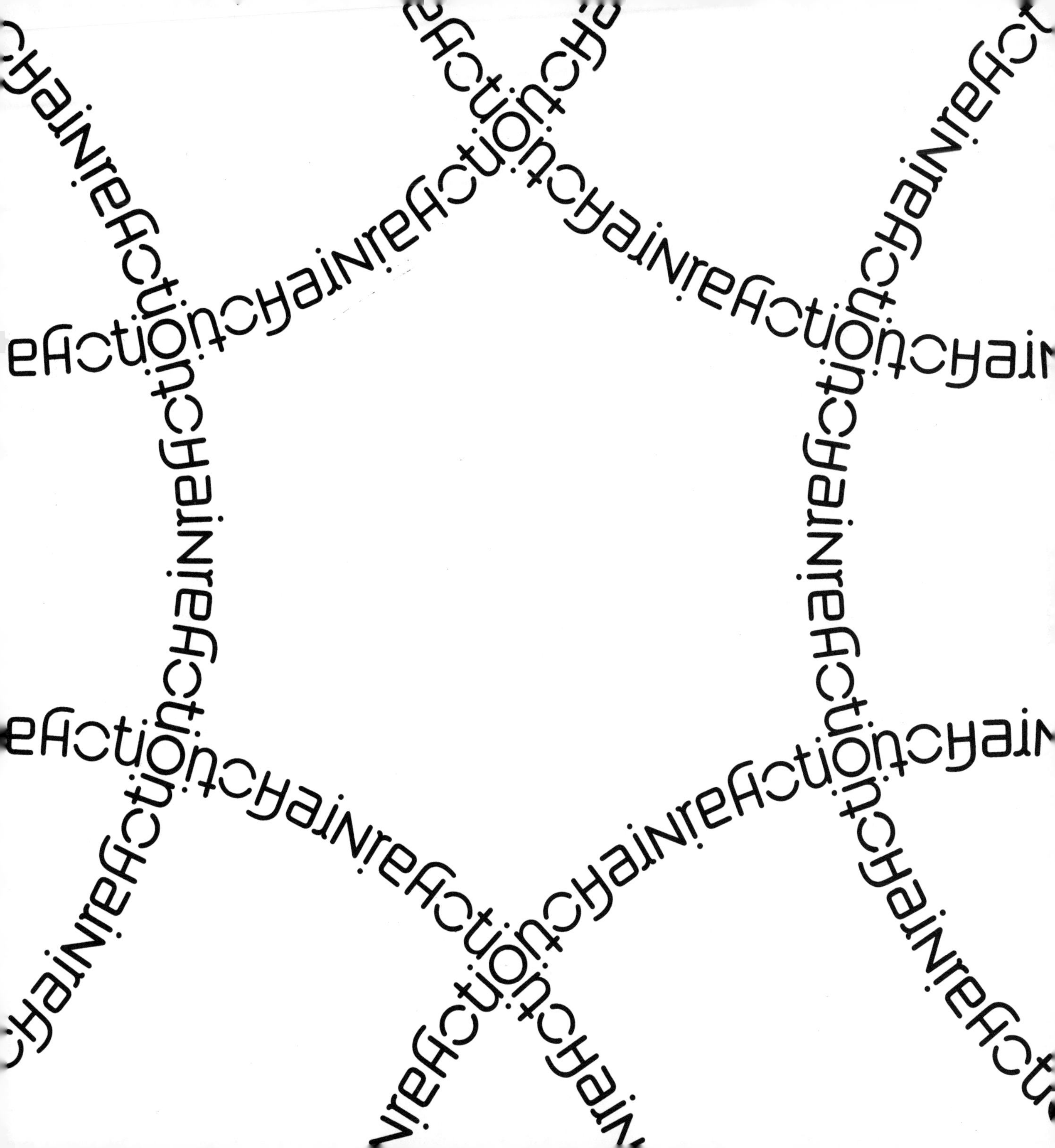
chainreaction

Energy

Few of us can fully comprehend the idea that $E = mc^2$. Nevertheless, *energy* is a dynamic word whose different common meanings are used fairly equally in our culture. An energetic person can perform a great deal of work. We use our energy resources to effect change in our lives: to light and heat our homes and to move ourselves from one place to another. No matter what the situation, nothing is accomplished without the transfer of energy.

One of the most significant aspects of energy, recognized particularly since Einstein established its relationship to mass, is that it cannot be created or destroyed. The amount of energy present at the Big Bang (which must have been a lot, given what's come of it) still exists in its various forms throughout the universe. These include electricity, heat, light, sound, chemical energy, and mass, which are all interchangeable. It is by transforming from one form to another that energy gets things done.

My lava lamp demonstrates a chain reaction that involves several of these forms and changes. The power company may transform mass, in the form of fossil fuels (which once were living organisms deriving their energies from the heat and light of the sun and the consumption of other organisms), to heat and then electricity. When I plug the lava

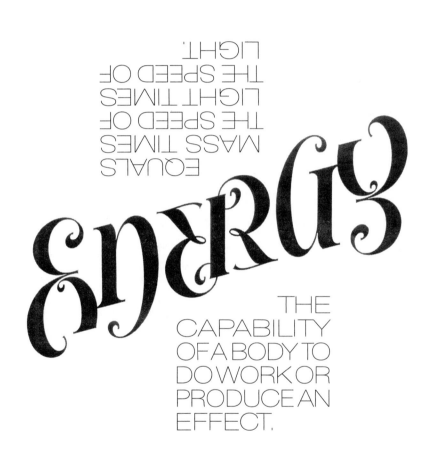

ENERGY

EQUALS MASS TIMES THE SPEED OF LIGHT TIMES THE SPEED OF LIGHT.

THE CAPABILITY OF A BODY TO DO WORK OR PRODUCE AN EFFECT.

lamp in and turn the switch from off (yin) to on (yang), the electrical energy is converted to the heat and light of the light bulb. The red goopy stuff (to use the precise scientific name) in the bottom of the conical vessel is heated, which diminishes its density and softens it. As its density becomes less than that of the oil it lives in, it rises. The light adds to the visual appeal of the undulating goop and helps to stimulate my brain cells. I then have more energy to apply to whatever task is on my desk. But I'm not sure that this last transfer of energy follows the mathematical formulas that apply to the other transformations.

A pendulum swings to and fro, shuttling back and forth from east to west. In the West, pendulums are perceived to go "tick, tock," but in the East they go "yin, yang, yin, yang . . ." The ebb and flow of the pendulum is symbolic of many harmonic, complementary relationships. The pendulum can also function as a model for a more subtle yin and yang relationship: the inverse ratio that exists between two common forms of energy—potential energy and kinetic energy.

Potential energy, as its name implies, is energy that is not currently active but exists due to the position of the body in question. A boulder sitting in the middle of a flat plain has little likelihood of going anywhere and therefore has little potential energy. But the same boulder perched at the edge of a cliff, patiently waiting for one or two more grains of sand to be eroded away before it plummets into the gorge below, has great potential energy.

Kinetic energy is energy that an object has due to its motion and is in proportion to its mass and velocity. Once the boulder falls, it has plenty of kinetic energy.

This photograph was taken on the north shore of the upper arm of Cape Cod in the vicinity of Brewster, Massachusetts. The unique topography of the area has created tidal flats, gradually sloping expanses that are underwater at high tide and exposed as undulating beach at low tide. As the tides change, alternating strips of sand and water are created, revealing what is, in effect, a fleeting but relatively stationary replication of wave pattern.

The **LIGHT/DARK** chain ambigram, with light split into its component colors of the spectrum.

The **AMBIGUITY** ambigram, taken to extremes.

**QUOTH THE RAVEN,
'NEVERMORE.'**

The refrain from Edgar
Allan Poe's amazing poem
"The Raven" is repeated 8
times in this print, or an
infinite number of times if
you choose to keep read-
ing either clockwise or
counterclockwise. Poe
occasionally indulged in a
form of wordplay in which
the sound at the end of
one word is repeated
immediately at the begin-
ning of the following word.
By running those sounds
together, Poe created a
more fluid line of poetry.
By eliminating the aurally
redundant *th* (quo*th the*)
and *n* (rave*n n*evermore),
I was able to create the
ambigram.

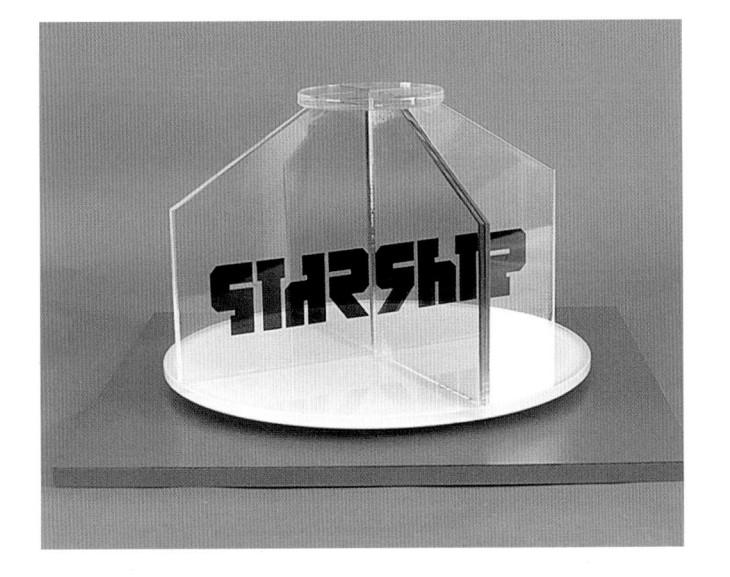

The **Starship** ambigram has bilateral (mirror-image) symmetry. The ambigram was screen-printed onto a shaped piece of glass that is inter-sected at the midpoint by a two-sided mirror. Perfect 360-degree symmetry is the result, with STARSHIP being readable from any vantage point. Ambigram designed for Jefferson Starship in 1975. Turntable sculpture designed for, and con-structed by, the Franklin Institute, Philadelphia, Pennsylvania.

The **Transparent** ambi-gram is also designed to have bilateral symmetry. Here the ambigram has been etched into one side of heavy glass, which is edge-lit from below. The incised letters catch the light, making the ambi-gram readable from both sides. Glasswork by Luc Century, Sanibel, Florida.

WHOLENESS.
Enamel on canvas,
12 in. diameter, 1997.
The word *hole* has been
designed as a rotational
ambigram and repeated
at 90 degrees to form a
mandala-like balance,
which suggests a com-
pletion, or wholeness.

Collection of Conni James.

EDUCATION.
Enamel and chalk on canvas,
18 x 28 in., 2000.
An "oscillation" ambigram. There is no symmetry here other than the complementary relationship between teaching and learning. The illusion depends on the willingness of the viewer to see the letterforms as ambiguously spelling out either *teach* or *learn*.

Us. Oil on canvas,
30 x 20 in., 1998.
The "me" and "you" fig-
ure/ground ambigram is
rendered as a solid, finite
form in an infinite space.
This recalls Alan Watts'
contention that he some-
times felt as though he
were yang and the rest of
the universe were yin.

A PORTRAIT OF THE ARTIST.
Oil and acrylic on canvas,
44 x 44 in., 1996.
Several layers of Joycean
(and Langdonian) word-
play surround this
figure/ground ambigram.
Among these are refer-
ences to the male (and
overt) name "James" and
the female (and covert)
name "Joyce," and a
reunification of the bifur-
cated sentence that
begins and ends
Finnegans Wake.

OPTICAL ILLUSION.
Oil on canvas,
18 x 48 in., 1999.
This figure/ground ambi-
gram reminds the viewer
that all representational
painting creates the optical illusion of three-
dimensional space on a
two-dimensional surface.

THE PERSISTENCE OF INFLUENCE.
Oil on canvas,
44 x 44 in., 2000.
The figures arranged from left to right across the ground spell out the first name of one of my favorite painters, while his last name can be read in the spaces left between those objects. The painting is a humble imitation of, and an homage to, one of my earliest and strongest influences, Salvador Dalí.
Collection of Melba Pearlstein.

IMAGINATION (GREEN).
Enamel on paper,
22 x 11 in., 1998.
Rorschach print,
bilateral symmetry.

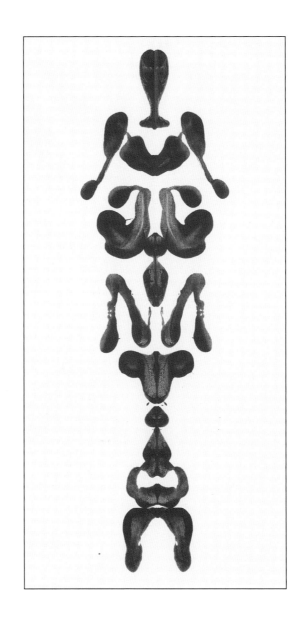

FORWORDS.

Latex enamel on canvas, 36 x 18 in., 2001.

The first of a new series of paintings, *FORWORDS* goes back to ambigram square one. It begins with the simple word *no* which, when inverted, becomes *on*. Both words suggest their three-letter opposites, and four words are the result.

AMBIGUITY.
Latex enamel on canvas,
36 x 72 in., 2003.
Another take on my
favorite theme. The series
that began with *FORWORDS*
did not repeat the
inversion motif but has
continued to exploit the
concept of complemen-
tary opposites.

THE ROADWAY.
Mixed media,
c. 30 in. diameter,
c.1986.
The essence of getting
from point A to point B
in space or time is
"the way," "the path"—
or the road. The essence
is the Tao.

In its lateral path, the pendulum possesses and exerts both forms of energy. At the extreme ends of its arc, it comes to a complete, if imperceptible, stop. At that point, the pendulum has no kinetic energy but has attained its maximum potential energy. Instantly, as that potential begins to be realized, its potential energy decreases, but it does not instantly disappear. At every point until it reaches its lowest point, in the center of the arc, its position renders it still subject to the force of gravity, and thus it maintains a degree of potential energy. Throughout the course of the pendulum's descent to its lowest point its speed increases, and so proportionately does its kinetic energy. At its lowest point, the pendulum has no potential energy; its position alone would get it nowhere. But since its velocity will begin to decrease as it passes its nadir, it is, at that moment, going as fast as it will go in the course of its arcing path. Therefore, having fallen to the bottom of its arc, the pendulum possesses its maximum kinetic energy.

In a symmetrical manner, the pendulum's kinetic energy then decreases and its potential energy increases as it climbs to the opposite high point. There, once again, its kinetic energy will momentarily cease to exist, while its potential energy enjoys a brief moment of maximum power.

In a thermal rather than a strictly mechanical system, the goop in the lava lamp goes through similar changes. The heat it takes on while at rest at the bottom indirectly gives it a kind of kinetic energy, which elevates it to the top of the vessel. There it rests in a state of potential energy again while it cools and its density increases. It then succumbs to the force of gravity and falls to the bottom. There the goop begins the process again, ever changing, falling as yin falls, rising as yang rises.

Action/Re-action

It is interesting to find that the laws of physics often seem to apply to human behavior as well. Following what must originally have been an instinct for fairness, ancient codes of morality called for "an eye for an eye, and a tooth for a tooth." A crime was seen as an unsettling of the natural balances in life, and justice was an attempt by human beings to restore those balances by a punishment that fit the crime—an equal and opposite reaction. Most early societies accepted this approach as right and proper. Later, the principles of Christianity introduced the idea of forgiveness—"turning the other cheek." While this seems, on the face of it, to be an advance in human development, we should not overlook the fact that at the same time, religions that had abandoned the Earth Mother and other nature-oriented gods and goddesses were beginning to predominate, as they do today. As this more modern mode of religious thought accompanied the development of Western civilization, which in time gained its predominance in the world, human beings began to believe that their new religious principles were superior to those of more primitive societies, and also that mankind was separate from and superior to nature itself. The technologies that Western cultures developed have supported this idea and helped to fulfill the biblical directive for man to "have dominion over the earth." We now realize that, taken to their logical extremes, the prac-

TO EVERY

ACTION

THERE IS
ALWAYS
OPPOSED
AN EQUAL

RE-

ACTION

SIR ISAAC
NEWTON

SIR ISAAC
NEWTON

THERE IS
ALWAYS
OPPOSED
AN EQUAL

TO EVERY

tices associated with this attitude would destroy the conditions upon which mankind's existence depends. Nature would eventually exact its form of appropriate retribution—the extinction of mankind. The wrongs would then be punished, the balance restored. An eye for an eye.

This is not to blame the Judeo-Christian tradition entirely for our present environmental problems. Nor is it to say that, in order to live more naturally and responsibly, we must go back to the "eye for an eye" approach to justice. The idea of forgiveness is not necessarily at odds with the natural law of action and reaction.

Some scholars believe that Jesus' teachings were influenced by the principles of Hinduism and Buddhism. These religions, which developed in India several centuries before the birth of Christ, shared the concept of karma—literally, "doing"—which is linked to the idea of reincarnation. The sum of one's actions in each lifetime is carried on into the next life, where one's status is determined by the quality of the soul's karma. If a person performs evil acts, even if they go unpunished in his current lifetime, his entire next life will be affected by the negative energy of that karma. So a judge or jury of one's peers is not necessary in order to bring about an equal and opposite reaction, and thus, forgiveness in this life has a place.

We need not believe in the Buddhist or Hindu doctrine of reincarnation, however, in order to make use of the idea of karma. Jesus taught that one's reward would come in the "afterlife" (a subtle shift from one's "next life") and that God, not man, would be the judge of a person's actions. We may also believe that one's karma takes its toll upon the evil-doer internally, within the same lifetime, and that the wrong done has a greater deleterious effect on the doer than it does on the one to whom it is done. No matter how we look at it, what goes around, comes around.

Perfection

A circle simultaneously displays characteristics that are both finite and infinite. Iconographically speaking, the circle has long been used to represent perfection. It is both infinite and complete. This is undoubtedly a response and an homage to the inherent cycles that surround us. These cycles can be described in systems of symbols using mathematics, which, as the English philosopher Bertrand Russell put it, is "capable of a stern perfection," and mathematics may be about the only direct experience with perfection that we can have. But math itself is not a real thing. It is a language of theory, a way of discussing the ideal. By its very definition, perfection is not attainable. Our sensitivities and powers of perception tell us that nothing is perfect. How appropriate, then, that our mathematical symbol for nothing is a circle. Zero, while still something we can't really experience, is absolute. What else is? Only infinity, symbolically represented by another circuit.

All the same, perfection is a nice idea to have around as a carrot hanging at the end of our intellectual stick. The theoretical existence of perfection gives us something to shoot for, an elusively indefinite pi in the sky. We can improve ourselves and our efforts forever. "The indefatigable pursuit of an unattainable perfection . . . is what alone gives a meaning to our life on this unavailing star," wrote British essayist Logan

Pearsall Smith. Similarly, an Episcopal minister once told my religion class, "Religion is what makes sense out of the senselessness of our lives." And indeed, one of the more familiar symbolic uses of the circle is found in Christian decorative arts, where it represents God.

Mineral crystals are among the most discernible examples of perfection in nature. In their various structures, classified according to the type of symmetry they exhibit, crystals adhere to obvious mathematical rules. Our fascination with them is understandable. They invite us in, saying, "Look close. There *is* order. Things *do* make sense." They are a hint— nature's way of telling us that our mathematical and scientific systems are on the right track.

In many ways crystals are like us. No two are exactly alike; each is beautiful in its own way. We can relate to them on an emotional level because, like us, each has its flaws. Without the flaws, crystals would look like a piece of manufactured plastic. Perfection and emotion do not go hand in hand.

The curious among us are never happy accepting an idea on one level when it may be explored and expanded to further dimensions, and our fixation with the circle as a symbol of the ideal takes on greater depth in 3-D. The sphere is symbolic of the orb we live on and is idealized in the most mystical of all crystals, the crystal ball. The perfection of all crystals can instill a sense of calm, and the sphere may do this best of all. Concentration can produce a meditative effect, and in that state the mind of a "seer" can freely associate the shapes and patterns created by the imperfections of the crystal to the patterns of life and, some might say, the shape of things to come.

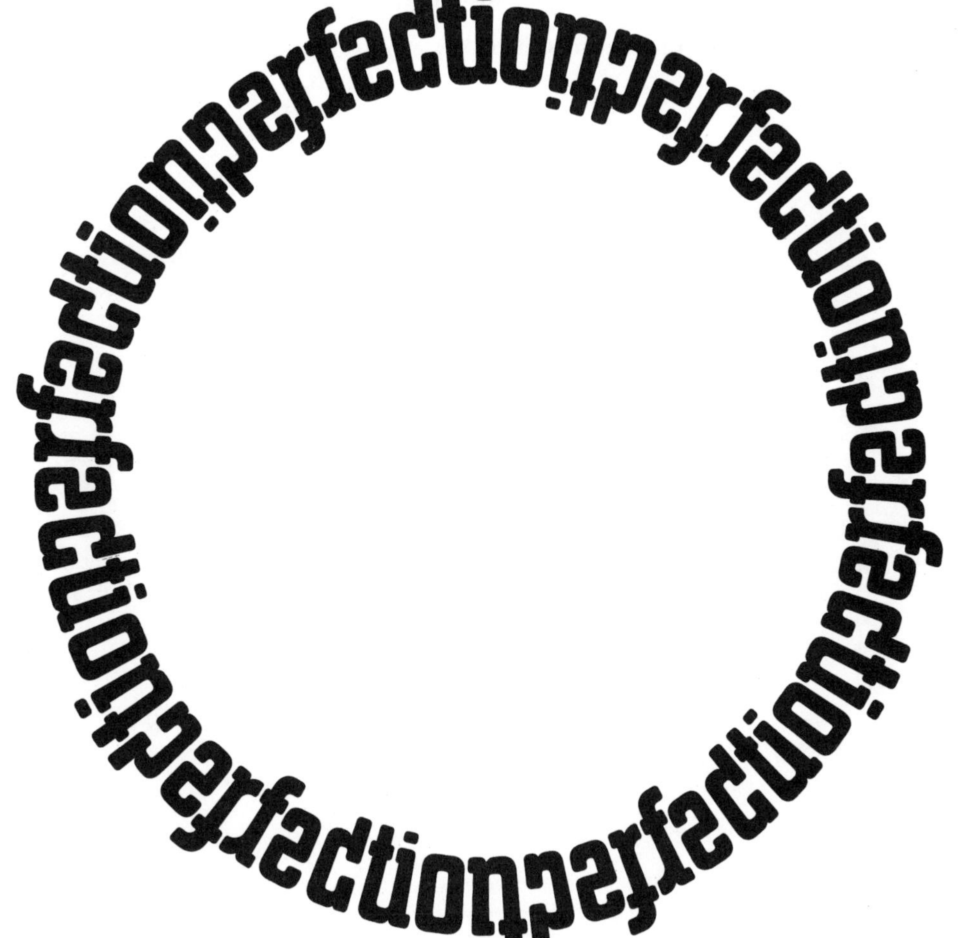

perfectionperfectionperfectionperfectionperfectionperfectionperfectionperfection

What is always predictable, but no clairvoyant will ever report, is death, the eternal infinite. Many religions, on the other hand, predict that death brings the attainment of perfection. One's life comes full circle. It is complete. Robert Browning wrote, "What's come to perfection perishes." But it works the other way around as well.

Mathematics

Mathematics is a coded language through which we can tell the gods that we are not unaware of what is going on around us. Or it may be the most self-flattering, self-aggrandizing trivia game ever invented. Bertrand Russell seems to have seen these two points of view. He wrote that mathematics "possesses not only truth, but supreme beauty—a beauty cold and austere . . . yet sublimely pure" and also that math "may be defined as the subject in which we never know what we are talking about, nor whether what we are saying is true."

We have found about a zillion ways of dressing up the equal sign. You can put x on one side and $\frac{-b \pm \sqrt{b^2 - 4ac}}{2a}$ on the other. You can put E on the left and mc^2 on the right, or 1 on one side and 1 on the other. To really go wild, you can say that if $a = b$ and $b = c$, then $a = c$. You can add $(5 + 5 = 10)$, subtract $(5 - 5 = 0)$, multiply $(5 \times 5 = 25)$ and divide $(5/5 = 1)$. Do with numbers what you will, it all comes down to the equal sign. The rest is symmetry, of a sort.

Did human beings always know that they had the same number of digits (!) on both their left and right hands? And the same on each foot? I prefer to think that one day, not too shortly after the dawn of homo sapiens, one individual came running back to the cave with that exciting discovery. "How obvious," we think. Then later: "E = mc²!" "How obvious," the gods think.

"There's a divinity that shapes our ends, rough-hew them how we will," said Hamlet. There *is* an order to the universe, and starting with the person who discovered the symmetries of the extremities, and continuing through the present with formulators of theories about "strings," galactic bubbles, DNA, dark matter, and white holes, we human beings understand some percentage of that order. *Divinity,* as Shakespeare wrote the word, with a lowercase *d,* could be interpreted as "divine-ness," not necessarily as "God." What could be more divine than the fact that Norfolk Island pines, sunflowers, lizards, and snowflakes use the same mathematical system we do. It's enough to make a person feel like part of the system.

The early Taoist philosophers must have sensed that human beings are part of the system. Their observations of nature guided their principles and their approach to life. But their focus was as much on the concept of opposition as on the idea of equality. The Taoists may or may not have been impressed that $5 = 5$, or even that $2 + 3 = 5$. Symbolically speaking, they focused on the fact that the numbers in question were on *opposite sides* of the equals sign. Observing the sun and moon, man and woman, night and day, they concluded that opposites were equal and in balance.

The graphic inspiration of the equal sign is not terribly well disguised: two separate elements of identical length and thickness—two things that are equal. The gods may have been satisfied when we real-

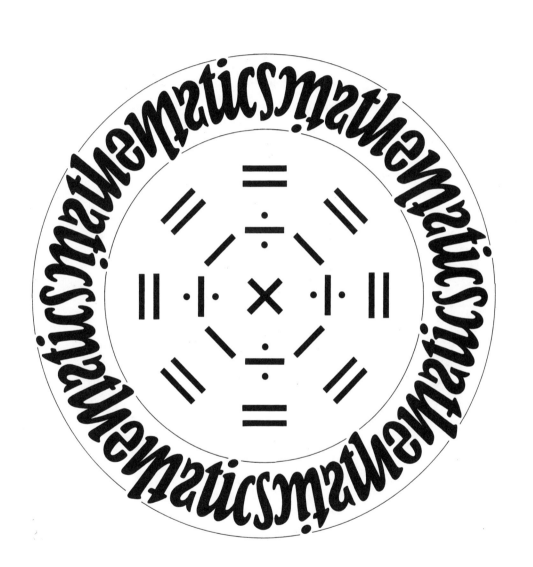

ized that things that appeared to be different could actually be the same. After all, we don't seem to have progressed very far beyond that theme.

Every scientific proof depends on that balance. Every piece of art in some way responds to the concept of repetition and variation. Things are different, yet ultimately the same. Chaos, according to the Bible, is what *preceded* creation. What follows is its opposite—order.

Is chaos then equal to order? Yes, in that they are the two states in which we are able to imagine the existence of all things. If they are equal, maybe one didn't simply supplant the other forever. Perhaps they alternate. Does order then depend on awareness?

In any case, mathematics is our security blanket. As long as we have it, we can feel that our lives make sense, rough-hew them how we may.

Mathematics is not about numbers so much as it is a way of thinking, a way of framing questions that allows us to turn things inside out and upside down to get a better sense of their true nature.

The Universe and the Teacup: The Mathematics of Truth and Beauty,

K. C. Cole

Algebra

The fact that the root of the word *algebra* means the "redintegration," or reuniting, of broken parts is intriguing when looked at through yin and yang lenses. Yin and yang, after all, also form a union of separate parts.

In trying to figure out how *algebra* came to be the name of a branch of mathematics, I first needed a definition of the word as we use it today. Algebra is the area of mathematics that focuses on relationships between numbers, using letters to help solve equations and establish the value of unknown quantities. Let's look at an example:

$$5x + 3 = 2x + 15$$

Now we don't know right away what the value of x is, but by first getting all the unknown (yin) entities on one side and the known (yang) numbers on the other, we can figure it out pretty easily.

$$5x - 2x = 15 - 3$$
$$3x = 12$$
$$x = 4$$

Plugging that back into the original equation, we find that

$$(5 \times 4) + 3 = (2 \times 4) + 15$$
$$\text{or } 23 = 23$$

Voilà! Redintegration!

Apparently the broken parts had fallen on both sides of the equal sign, and only when the separate quantities of *x* are reunited, the value of *x* is established.

Now for an unannounced, open-book quiz that was developed by a frequently puzzling friend, Scott Kim. This is a test. Had it been an actual alert, you would have been instructed to report back to ninth grade. Repeat: This is only a test.

Solve for *x:*

1. XLGEBRX

2. xray = black + white

3. 2*x* or not 2*x.* That is the question.

4. (9 + 7*x*/2 = (4 - 2*x* (6 - 2*x*

5. Drifxod

6. $ = mxy

7. Solve: (hint: "When in Rome . . .")

  n1ne

  sk2ng

  f4e

  se5en

  mo6ng

  s9

  e10it

algebra is the branch of mathematics in which symbols subdue the fear of the unknown is derived from an Arabian word: "AL-JEBR" — the redintegration of broken parts

Big Bang

The universe seems to be expanding, still expending the energy of the Big Bang. Its momentum continues. But there are hypotheses that that momentum will eventually dissipate and the universe will then begin to retrace its steps and eventually collapse, perhaps as totally and dramatically as it began. Yang followed by yin. Perhaps yin will be followed by another yang event: Big Bang II (if indeed our self-centered view of cosmology is correct that the Big Bang was the first of its kind), ultimately followed by a wavelike series of expansions and contractions.

A black hole is thought to be a massive star whose nuclear energy has been exhausted. Its outward thrust of energy thus diminished, it shrinks. Succumbing to its own gravity, its mass becomes increasingly dense. The resulting gravitational pull is so great that it not only accumulates more mass in the form of any matter within its gravitational field, it also pulls light and even space toward it as well. A black hole may or may not continue in that state forever, but it seems possible that it could reach a critical mass and explode, creating what is known as a "white hole." Could the Big Bang have been only the first in a series of expanding and contracting, exploding and imploding universes?

• • •

Chapter one of Genesis reports that "the earth was without form, and void; and darkness was upon the face of the deep." Many creation myths say the same thing, with light being created in short order. It doesn't seem to me that science and the Bible are in much disagreement. If a white hole did what it's theorized to do, it would probably look a good bit like the Big Bang. If the Big Bang had been the product of a black hole, it would probably have had all the available light tucked inside it, though possibly in the form of mass or some other form of energy. And an explosion of that magnitude can hardly be imagined without light as a product. If *all* matter were contained in that particular black hole, there would be hardly any need for space, since space is what comes between matter, so it would have to have brought its own space with it. The void that preceded the Big Bang is probably what's beyond the universe, but we may as well speculate as to what *we* were like before *we* were conceived. We can know our own lives. We can talk about the Big Bang. We may even someday know the universe, but as Lao-tzu says in *The Way of Lao-tzu,* "The tao that can be told of is not the eternal Tao."

Astronomy

In the same way that Alan Watts saw himself as yang and the rest of the universe as yin, so the earth could be yang and the rest of the universe yin. We tend to think of the rest of the universe as "other." We're here, and everything else is out there. Is this geocentric attitude arrogant? Imagine a grass seed, flung out with 35,813 others, saying to itself, "I'm special. There's nothing out there but grass seed. I'm the only one that can think."

We have no idea whether there are other sentient beings in the universe or not. Given the peculiar set of circumstances to which we owe our existence, the odds against a recurrence of those factors would seem to be astronomical. On the other hand, given the infinite scope of the universe, what are the odds that anything could happen only once? Is the universe, like pi, a mathematically irrational system within which nothing repeats? Or is it like a fraction that does repeat but hasn't been divided out far enough to find the refrain? The nighttime sky has attracted the attention of earthlings for at least as long as humans have been around. Our curiosity, our compulsion to understand our circumstances appears to be as infinite as the universe.

Plato said, "Astronomy compels the soul to look upwards and leads us from this world to another." I'd put it another way. Our soul compels astronomy to look upwards and lead us from this world to another.

IS THE STUDY OF ALL THE BODIES OF THE
UNIVERSE. IT HAS ALLOWED US TO SEE THE
EARTH FROM A DIFFERENT POINT OF VIEW.

Astronomy

"COMPELS THE SOUL TO LOOK UPWARDS AND
LEADS US FROM THIS WORLD TO ANOTHER."

Syzygy

A number of the words portrayed in this book have more than one meaning. It is appropriate that there is more than one way to regard these words linguistically as well as visually. In the cases of *inertia* and *ambiguity,* the two meanings can even seem to be opposite, polarized at 180 degrees, just as the two visual vantage points are—and yin and yang are also. Oddest of all perhaps is *syzygy.* Its two meanings are different and yet not opposite, but at an angle to each other. According to the *Columbia Encyclopedia* (fourth edition), a syzygy is the "alignment of three bodies of the solar system along a straight or nearly straight line." (A *nearly* straight line might connect the word *syzygy* with its two meanings.) The *Oxford English Dictionary* gives the Greek word for yoke, or pair, as the root of *syzygy* and then says [emphasis added], "conjunction and opposition of *two* heavenly bodies," and later, "the conjunction of *two* organisms without loss of identity" (yin and yang's favorite), and still farther along says, "a pair of connected or correlative things . . . a couple or pair of opposites." The word *three* does not appear anywhere in the list. Nowhere in the encyclopedia definition is the word *two* mentioned. What's up here?

One of the most vexing truths of science is that no phenomenon can be investigated without taking into account the presence of the investi-

SYZYGY

THE JOINING OF
TWO ENTITIES,
WITHOUT LOSS
OF IDENTITIES.

gator. Herein lies the disparity between the definitions: the *OED*'s definition leaves out the observer. The *Columbia* includes the Earth (presumably as a vantage point) in each of its examples. But the *OED* redeems itself in its definition of *opposition,* a concept mentioned by both sources in defining *syzygy.* Opposition in astronomy, it says, is "the relative position of two heavenly bodies when exactly opposite to each other *as seen from the earth's surface . . .* [emphasis added]."

Ironically, with the added element of the observer's vantage point, it could be argued that syzygy has rendered itself meaningless as a concept. If it can be accepted that the Earth is an arbitrary vantage point (are astronauts forbidden to use the word *syzygy?),* then any vantage point, at least in the solar system, should be okay. If that is the case, any three heavenly bodies can be brought into syzygy, simply by choosing the proper planet or moon to stand on.

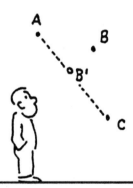

The observer in the diagram is looking at the same three stars as we are—A, B, and C—but from a different place. His position is in a plane with the stars; ours is perpendicular to that plane. Whereas we do not see A, B, and C as being aligned, the observer does because he sees star B as if it were in the B' position.

The ancient Greeks apparently did not use the word *syzygy* to describe astronomic positions. In the early eighteenth century, when the word was adopted for that purpose, it must have been taken for granted that heavenly bodies could be viewed from only one vantage point—the Earth. Therefore any apparent coupling, or lineup, of two bodies in space necessarily included a third—the one upon which the observer stood.

In any case, the "syzygy" ambigram rises to the occasion and sets the mind at ease. It satisfies both points of view. It is readable from two diametrically opposite points, and thus yokes them together. So the ambigram is a syzygy, any way you look at it.

Limits / Infinity

The stages of one human being's life may be compared to the stages of development of human beings in general. The awareness of our environment increases as time goes by. Infants are probably aware, at first, only of mother, then other family members and home. Subsequent experience expands awareness to neighborhood and then to town. In time, more theoretical learning brings us in touch with our country, the world, and beyond, into the solar system and the universe. Eventually, in many cases, the process repeats itself in reverse, awareness diminishing as death approaches.

Throughout most of human history, people have understood and accepted limits. Primitive humans must have spent their whole lives acquainted with only a tiny part of the world. No one in the history of the village had ever been across the river or traversed the mountain range in the distance. Life was demanding enough right there in the valley. Those with the curiosity to wonder what lay beyond the horizon or the frontier were often considered dreamers or worse and sometimes subjected to all manner of abuse. But curiosity persists as a driving human force, and as individual curiosities are pursued and satisfied, subsequent cultural acceptance has allowed many old limitations to fall.

As technology develops to catch up with and satisfy curiosity, cul-

tural awareness grows. In 1609, Galileo developed the first telescope used to survey the heavens. He may also have been the inventor of the microscope, which was first used at around the same time. Any number of times since then, scientists have thought that they had reached a limit—in terms of the imaginable size of the universe or the amount of material in it and, in the other direction, the smallest units of matter. In time, each has been exceeded.

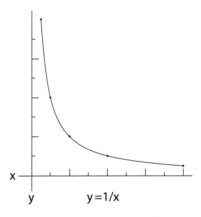

x

y $y = 1/x$

The various natural systems that display themselves in mathematical terms often reveal nature's response to limits, usually demonstrating the principle of "approaching [but never reaching] zero as a limit." The purest and most abstract rendition of this concept would be a graph of the equation $y = 1/x$, resulting in a hyperbolic curve. Each leg of this curve will continue to get closer to the coordinate nearest it, as long as further values for x are determined. But like a microbe jumping from its original position halfway to a wall, then jumping halfway again, the limit of the coordinate will never be reached.

infinity

A NEVERENDING LINE THAT REPRESENTS AN UNREACHABLE POINT AT THE END OF

Although it is apparently growing in size, most astrophysicists now believe that the universe is finite. But the human mind with its apparently limitless curiosity, in an attempt to comprehend a finite universe, says, "Yeah, well, what's beyond it?" Some say the concept of infinity is hard to grasp. But in some ways, it now seems harder to comprehend limitations.

It is our understanding of the word *limits* that's a problem. What we have considered limits in the past were only milestones or boundaries. These can be passed and crossed. Ultimately, limits are what we can approach but never reach. And we can do that for an infinite amount of time. It may very well be that the finite and the infinite are the same thing or are definitively braided together. Could yin exist without yang?

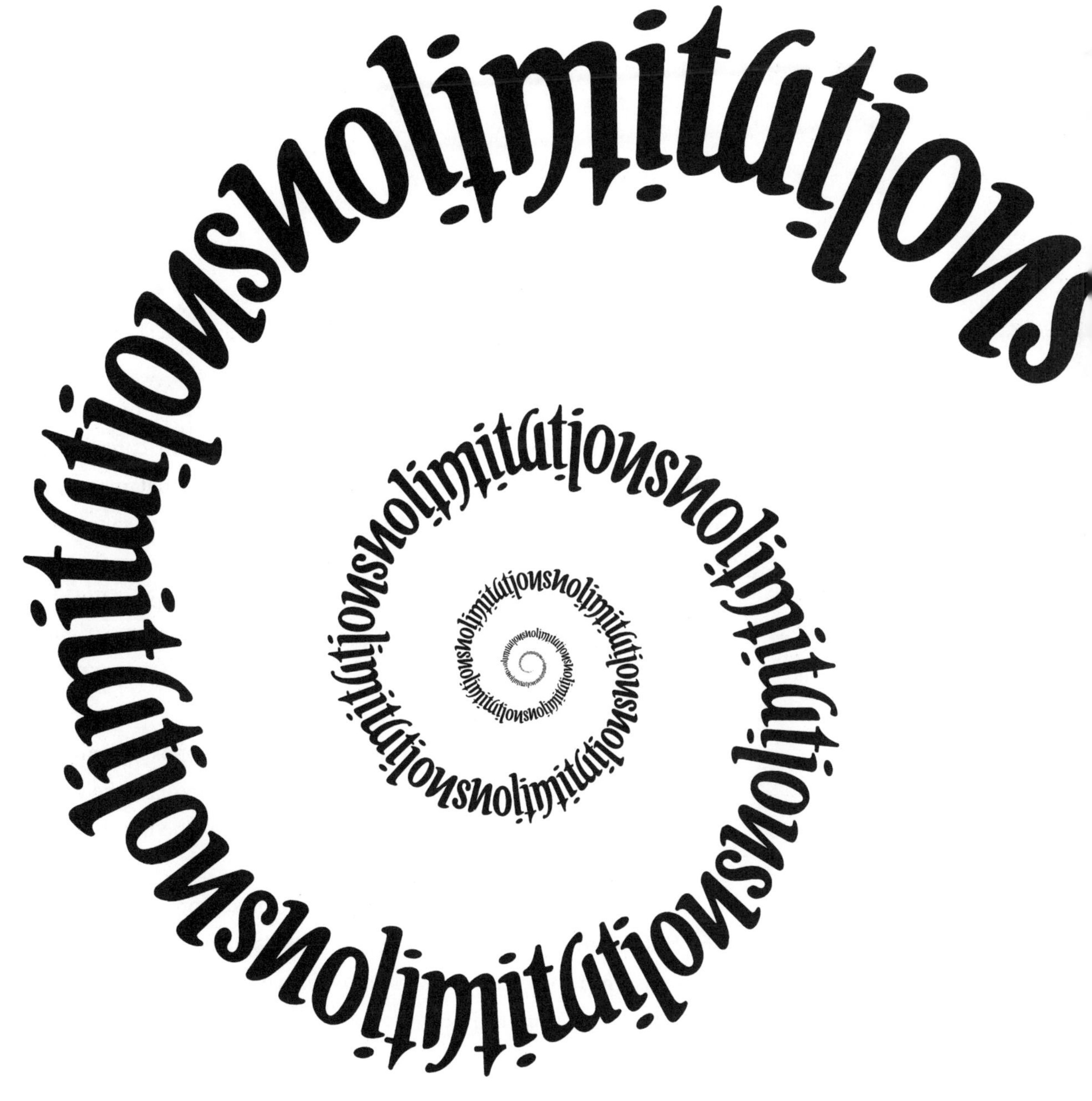
nolimitations

Spirals

History doesn't repeat itself, but it rhymes.

Ascribed to both Will Rogers and Mark Twain

Is existence linear or cyclical? An argument could be made either way. Some things, it seems, will never return. I'm counting on never having to take trigonometry again or, for that matter, repeating *any* of my adolescence. And so far we don't see dinosaurs coming around every now and then. Are they gone forever or are they just on a slower schedule than, say, Halley's comet or wide lapels? But then there are other things like political campaigns, paying bills, and doing laundry that roll around so predictably that they may very well have their own sighting niches at Stonehenge.

Whenever strong support can be made for two opposing points of view, it's a pretty good bet that both are true. Or, as physicist Niels Bohr put it, "The opposite of a shallow truth is false. But the opposite of a deep truth is also true."

Thesis and antithesis are no more than polarized opposites without the unifying force of synthesis. Yin is yin, and yang is yang, even if they are across the room from each other. Yet it's hard to know what they are and what they mean until they are joined. So yes, existence is both lin-

A SPIRAL IS A CONTINUOUSLY CURVING LINE TRAVELING IN THREE DIMENSIONS AROUND & ALONG THE AXIS OF A CONE OR CYLINDER AT A REGULAR RATE.

spirals

A SPIRAL IS A CONTINUOUSLY CURVING LINE MOVING IN TWO DIMENSIONS AROUND A FIXED POINT AT A STEADILY DECREASING OR INCREASING DISTANCE.

Mantra. Steel coils in wooden box, 1986.

To date, my only three-dimensional ambigram is this representation of the Sanskrit mantra *om*. The two letters in the sculpture are made from identical sections of steel coil. A little research into the meaning of the sound (its significance seems to be more as a sound than a word, per se) reveals a great number of interpretations, but all of them seem to converge toward a sense of oneness with the universe. Some describe the *o* sound and the *m* sound as representing complementary aspects

ear and cyclical. And the synthesis of this paradox is well represented by a spiral.

Spirals, in fact, synthesize the principles—and in many ways the graphic representations—of yin and yang (repetition and variation), infinity (a mathematically regular figure with no inherent end), and the normal bell curve and its graphic extension, a wave pattern (rising and falling). These relationships were explored more fully in the discussion of waves (pages 80 and 83), but it seems that, in fact, each one implies and encompasses all the others.

The only way I can imagine time as both linear and cyclical simultaneously is to represent it by way of a helix—the kind of spiral that winds its way around and along an imaginary cylinder. Looking at that helix from the end, one sees a circle. Viewing it from the side, the spring appears as a linear series of waves. Each morning, while coming at a predictable and repetitious time of day, is different from the one before and, presumably, the one to come. Every new moon, every January, appears at the same point on the circle, in a line with every one that preceded and is to come, and yet on a different point in the series of rising and falling waves of the helix.

The complexities and patterns of life can be seen

in this analogy by imagining a spring with a narrow diameter wrapped around the coil of a larger spring—in effect, a twisting cylinder. Imagine each spiral wrapped by a smaller spiral and in turn wrapped around a larger one. A spiral representing seconds encircles the minute coil sixty times for each revolution of the minute spiral, and the minute spiral does the same to the hour spiral. And on and on. We cannot even comprehend the sizes of the largest and smallest spirals, and, very likely, there aren't any such things. No end, no end.

of life, for instance a waking state and another level of consciousness. Some come close to an alpha and omega-like sense of beginning and ending—totality.

This treatment of the two letters as the same shape, repeated, would seem to complement those ideas. The two coils are diametrically opposed, literally, in that their diameters are at right angles to each other, and the two letters themselves approach almost the same level of oppositeness: the *o* (an inherently yin form) goes round and round, while the *m* (much more yang) goes up and down. The *o* is placid and soft, while the *m* is active and angular. The *o,* like an open mouth, is a passageway for the inhale and the exhale, while the rising and falling aspects of the *m* represent those breaths, and other such rhythms of existence.

Organic

S amuel Taylor Coleridge wrote, "The organic form . . . shapes, as it develops, itself from within, and the fullness of its development is one and the same with the perfection of its outward form." According to *Webster's Third New International Dictionary* of 1986, something organic has "distinct members or parts whose relations and powers or properties are determined by their function in the whole." It constitutes "a whole whose parts are mutually dependent or intrinsically related" and has "a form growing out of inherent factors (as function, site) rather than convention."

These quotations could just as well define and describe ambigrams. The letterform shapes, unlike those in conventional typography, develop from within each specific word and are not fully developed until the overall word, or outer form, has reached a state of "perfection," that is, attractiveness and readability. The letters are designed in such a way that their specific characteristics are based entirely on their position—their relationship to one another—within a specific word. In the design of a typeface, each letter is designed to read easily in juxtaposition with all fifty-one other capital and lowercase letters. This is an open system. The design of an ambigram, on the other hand, is a closed system. The letters are designed for one specific use, in direct relationship to the let-

HAVING THOSE PROPER-
TIES REQUIRED TO SUR-
VIVE AS A LIVING BEING.

orGanic

HAVING A STRUCTURE
THAT IS DESIGNED TO
PERFORM A FUNCTION.

ters on either side of it. That is why the *o* and the *c* in the "organic" ambigram are so different from the *o* and the *c* in "action/re-action." Ironically, the *g* and the *n* in "organic" *are* identical to the *g* and *n* in "magnetic." But recent studies have shown that on occasion there may be identical snowflakes as well.

Change/Changes

The car has been negotiating a long curve to the left, and you've adjusted your body weight so that leaning a little to your left keeps you from crushing your ribs into the door handle on your right. Then the road changes direction. Life is like that. Any road or process in life making its way from point A to point B has to weave its way around a few obstacles and must keep readjusting to stay oriented toward its destination. If the road goes up a hill, eventually it will come down. If it curves left, it will eventually curve right. Just when you feel that you have a handle on the way things are going and can relax a little, things change.

Some may think that it's a shame
that nothing ever stays the same,
that what is good and fine today
may soon become another way.
You just can't count on things to
stay the way they were just yesterday.
Seems contradictory and strange:
The only thing that's sure is change.

Stability is considered a personal attribute. And we often think of those who shake things up as troublemakers. It's true that most of us, to one degree or another, resist change. We seem to want the security of knowing what's likely to come. There has probably never been a time in human history when people have not sought the advice of oracles, astrologers, soothsayers, and palm, card, and tea leaf readers. But despite our apprehensions, without change we could scarcely know anything at

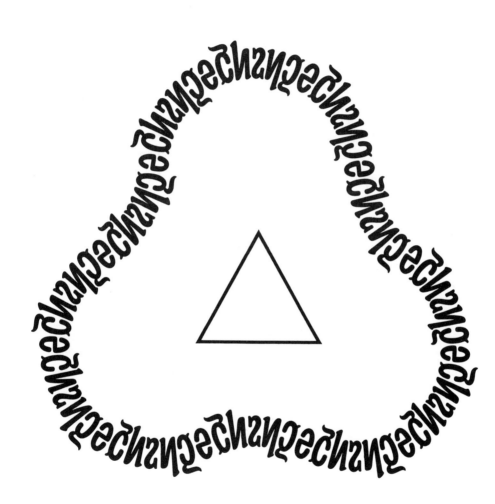

all. An incessant sound, whether the interior tintinnabulations some of us carry around in our ears or the exterior drone of crickets in the summertime, eventually becomes "white noise"—a perfectly audible sound that we do not hear. I'm told that the Hawaiian language has no word for weather since it changes so little there is no need to discuss it. I'd imagine that, confined for long enough in a bright red, empty cubicle, we'd lose the sense of redness—maybe even before we went completely mad. Without points of comparison, we couldn't know anything. The senses we depend on for information about our surroundings depend themselves on contrasts: light and shadow, hot and cold, high and low pitch and volume, the yins and the yangs of our environment.

The *I Ching,* or *Book of Changes,* is an ancient Chinese text of commentaries on a symbolic system that was intended to organize the complexities of life. The system was based on the dominant forces in nature, yin and yang. Chinese philosophers saw that nature was in a constant state of change as a result of the interaction of yin forces and yang forces, but they wanted to break that simplicity down into smaller increments in order to show greater relevance to everyday life. They surely felt there was an ebb and flow on a different scale than, say, summer and winter that could apply to the changes that occurred between Thursday and Friday.

The written form of yin was a broken (yielding) line, and of yang, an unbroken (unyielding) line:

Taking the two together produced yin and yang in union, but other pairs, called digrams, were possible as well:

Yang and yang, yin and yang, yang and yin, and yin and yin.

They were arranged as a suitably polarized and balanced whole:

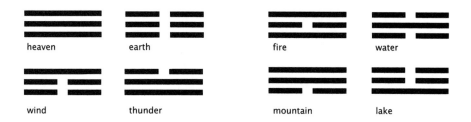

Continuing the process, trigrams came next, creating an octagon. The eight trigrams were named after major natural forces and elements, symbolically chosen for their "male" and "female" characteristics:

heaven   earth   fire   water

wind   thunder   mountain   lake

Ultimately the full pattern was realized when the trigrams were doubled, making sixty-four hexagrams and a virtual circle. This number allowed for all possible combinations of the eight primary natural symbols and was probably seen as being about as much complexity as anyone might need or could possibly comprehend.

The *I Ching* has been used as an oracle or fortune-teller through much of its history, but as with most predictors, its messages seem vague or oblique in their symbolic language. Obviously, reading that the fire brings warmth and the wind spreads the fire won't tell you whether to quit your job or not—at least not directly. The *I Ching* might say that the sun comes up out of the water and then evaporates it, in answer to the same question. What these pithy aphorisms do is to remind the seeker of the major forces in life, and the relationships referred to can then be applied to the situation at hand. The interpretation is supplied by the seeker. The same thing might be accomplished by choosing at random a spiral, the infinity symbol, a normal bell curve, or yin and yang, and laying that pattern over a given situation.

The *I Ching* is particularly fascinating, given the mathematical complexity derived from the simplicity of yin and yang. Equally compelling in understanding changes are the relationships between yin and yang, with the various Western incarnations of the symbol, and the virtually limitless number of situations that life may provide.

But change is movement. Change is growth.
Not bad or good, and yet it's both.
Our memories filled with days that passed
and brought us to today at last,
and still the moving shadows cast
*   ahead on what will be the past,*
as time moves on and rearranges;
an infinite amount of changes.

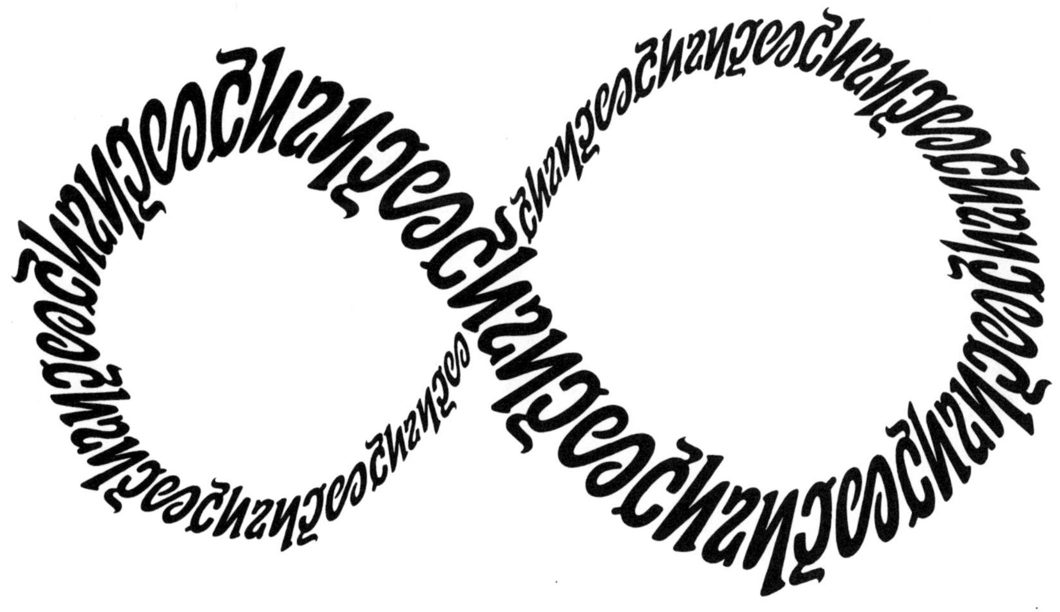

What we call the begining is often the end
And to make an end is to make a beginning.
The end is where we start from.

"Little Gidding," T. S. Eliot

NO END · NO END · NO END · NO END · NO END · NO END · NO END

neverendingneverendingneverendingneverendingneverending

eternaleternaleternaleternaleternaleternaleternal

The Origins and
History of My Ambigrams

Two factors are responsible for the fact that I create ambigrams: heredity and environment. My father's father was a poet and a linguist, and his mother was a fine art painter. They had died before I was born and I was unaware of those significant genetic influences until I was an adult. My father's beautiful penmanship came from that heritage. I was quite aware of that, and of my mother's rare indulgence in decorative painting and crafts. Those inherited gifts were powerful forces in shaping who I was to become, despite my being guided toward more conventional careers.

Life seems to make much more sense in retrospect than it does while it's unfolding, and so my earliest recollections of visual and verbal ambiguity seemed totally irrelevant when they happened. But a few of the significant ones have stuck in my mind.

Sometime in the late 1950s, my father took me to a football game. On one page of the program was this cartoon (re-created here from memory). I wanted to ask my dad whether the numbers had deliberately been drawn so they could be read as a word, but I knew that 7734 was a word you weren't supposed to say, so I never found out. On the other hand, it was publicly acknowledged that 1961 could be read as the same number no matter which way it was turned. That fact seemed more interesting to me than to most people.

Salvador Dalí, *Soft Construction with Boiled Beans: Premonition of Civil War.* Oil on canvas, 1936.

At around that time, I began to notice that the casual nature of cursive handwriting allowed for occasional ambiguity. Rather than overlook such mundane oddities, as most do, I took them in as opportunities for fun. No doubt, these were the kinds of discoveries that lured me away from the schoolwork I was supposed to be doing.

In a grade school art class I caught my first glimpse of Dalí's *Soft Construction with Boiled Beans: Premonition of Civil War.* It was probably the first painting I ever saw that was not a still life, a landscape, or a portrait.

Dalí became a lifelong influence, particularly for his figure/ground illusions, like the *Disappearing Bust of Voltaire.* But except for the cartoons that enhanced the margins of my textbooks, art remained in the background.

In college I discovered cubism, Escher, and the yin/yang symbol. And when, in my freshman year, the attendance requirements of an 8 A.M. (Tuesday, Thursday, and *Saturday)* History of Fine Art class proved to

Salvador Dalí, detail from *Slave Market with the Disappearing Bust of Voltaire*. Oil on canvas, 1940.

be a bit more demanding than I could manage, I became an English major. Shakespeare and History of the English Language awakened and nurtured my love of words.

I graduated with a degree in English and not a clue as to a direction in life. But I had begun to see myself as an artist—who just happened to have no art training to speak of.

Robert Indiana's 1966 *Love* painting seemed to anticipate the hippie movement, and as the Allman Brothers pointed out in 1970, "Love Is Everywhere." I loved and imitated psychedelic poster lettering, and the word *love* became an object of my graphic explorations, along with the yin/yang symbol. The following sketches (a couple of which are dated 1968) were culled from chaotic pages of doodles and drawings of all kinds, and compiled and organized a year or so later. They clearly show the embryonic stages of ambigrams.

With no idea how to become an artist, I naively looked for work in advertising and ended up in a related service industry, working in the photo-lettering darkroom of a type shop. At Walter T. Armstrong in Philadelphia, I learned a lot about type and saw the ad layouts that came in from the city's top advertising agencies.

Herb Lubalin, a leading graphic designer with a particular enthusiasm for the creative use of typography, was nearing the peak of his career in the early '70s. For years I wanted nothing more than to *become* him, and to do the kind of work he did. Graduating from the darkroom to the drawing board, I became proficient with a T square, triangle, and Rapidograph pen, and although I still had no idea how to become a professional logo designer, I started designing logos for my friends and coworkers. The one that I recall most clearly was my first rotationally symmetrical logo, done for Elizabeth Ann Stallone.

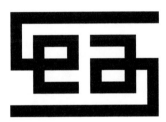

I began studying the best logos I could find in design publications, the most inspiring of which had been done by Tom Geismar, of Chermayeff and Geismar in New York City. I took some night school classes in drawing, painting, and advertising at the Pennsylvania Academy of Fine Art and the Philadelphia College of Art (now the University of the Arts).

At least once or twice a week, smoking pot with my friends or by myself, I put a pencil in my hand and a pad of paper on my lap and just let my mind wander and explore the graphic possibilities of the topics that occupied my mind: words, yin/yang relationships, and optical illusions. My inspiration for optical illusions at that time was M. C. Escher, whose

M. C. Escher's *"Sky and Water I."*

work explored symmetries, figure/ground relationships, and seeing the same thing from multiple viewpoints. I felt that there was a spiritual relationship between yin/yang and Escher's images, both graphically—the birds and fish fitting together as neatly as the yin and yang shapes—and conceptually, as he explored polarities like devils and angels, night and day, and more. Some of his pieces use reflection and inversion; some depict the same subject from different vantage points simultaneously. I began trying to do with words what Escher had done with birds and fish and buildings.

VISTA

By this time I had seen Raymond Loewy's NEW MAN design for a chain of French clothing stores, and Dick Hess' VISTA (Volunteers in Service to America) logotype. I was fascinated by their perfect rotational symmetry, but I was not immediately moved to imitate them, perhaps because the letters inverted so naturally, with so little manipulation. It must have seemed as though designs like those could happen only by way of rare coincidence. I was focused on forcing words into rotational figure/ground relationships. The results were, I felt, hard to read and quite unattractive.

Then late one night, I put on a great piece of music, lit a joint, opened

a new pad of Bienfang Graphics paper, a box of Marlboros, and a cold beer, sharpened a new Ticonderoga pencil, and sat down for a hour or so's worth of graphic exploration. Reflecting on the fact that I had everything a person such as myself could want, I wrote HEAVEN on the first page. The phone rang. I got up to answer it, and when I returned to my chair, I saw the word HEAVEN upside down and realized that I could design it the way the NEW MAN and VISTA logos had been done. Then I tried HELL, and then GOD. I felt that something very spiritual was going on.

HEAVEN   HELL GOD

As my orientation in those days was focused on logo design, I treated my ambigram sketches as studies for logotypes and executed them as finished "camera-ready" art.

HEAVEN HELL GOD

I began searching for words that would cooperate with my exciting discovery, running through the names of people I knew, the days of the week and months of the year. I had far more enthusiasm than ability or experience, but the sophistication of the logos I admired and the type-faces and type uses I had been exposed to held the threshold of success very high. Only a few words yielded to my efforts and achieved the standards I had set for typographic readability and harmonious aesthetics.

It was a major breakthrough when I realized that insisting that each letter become another when reversed, on a one-to-one basis, was very limiting, and that combining parts of letters facing one way could help create new letters facing the opposite direction. This idea may have been inspired by Lubalin's AVANT GARDE logotype and the typeface based on it, which featured unusual relationships where letters join or overlap.

The high percentage of words that refused to become ambigrams convinced me that there was little likelihood in their having a commercial application. It seemed that they could never be created on demand.

But they were too exciting to be ignored. By this time, I had become good friends with Bob Petrick, a dedicated painter who earned his living as a graphic designer. My enthusiasm for typography, logos, and ambigrams rubbed off on him, and soon Bob was creating ambigrams too. Our view of rock music as a countercultural, popular, and lucrative industry that both inspired and made use of highly innovative illustration and graphics led us to try to create ambigrams for the big stars and groups of the era. When the names worked, we tried mightily to penetrate the unappreciative layers of bureaucracy and protection that surrounded the stars. We succeeded in a very small number of cases. Bob sold this early ambigram to a group called

I tried again and again to wrestle the word *starship* into submission, but it resisted time after time. Finally I saw that it was perfectly willing to become an ambigram, if I would just open my mind to a different kind of symmetry. To date all of our attempts had been to create rotational ambigrams.

became the first mirror-image ambigram, as well as the first ambigram I was able to sell. It was used on the *Spitfire* album label, and in a number of applications in Jefferson Starship's 1976 tour, including an enormous banner stretched above the entire width of the stage. Or so I'm

told. My wife and I watched the group perform from onstage VIP seats. No one thought to tell us that we were sitting right beneath what is probably still the largest representation of an ambigram ever created.

But for all the challenge of creating an ambigram, it was still much harder to sell them. I continued to improve my ability to create ambigrams, working on any word, name, or project I could challenge myself with, but increasingly the question arose, "Why?"

Over the previous several years, my graphic explorations had not focused on words alone, but dwelt extensively on the yin/yang symbol. It had made a deep impression on me when I had first encountered it, but rather than research its origins and history, I constantly pulled it apart, reimagined and rebuilt it in pencil sketches on layout paper.

I mentally asked and graphically answered such questions as "What would happen if yin and then yang were each divided into yin and yang aspects?" "How would it look to view yin and yang from its edge?" "What if it had thickness?" and "What if many of them were piled on top of each other and what if it were three-dimensional instead of flat?" "What if I could animate the process as yin and yang evolved from the original image to one of those new forms, and then on to another?" Much to my surprise, other familiar symbols were revealed along the way: the normal bell curve, the infinity symbol, wave patterns, spirals and helixes.

Those revelations gave me a new list of words to try as ambigrams. And when some of them became successful ambigrams, it felt as if there was a strong resonance between the meaning of the word and its symmetrical graphic treatment. Even though there was no apparent outlet for the ambigrams, it felt as though there was a reason to create the

word BALANCE or POLARIZED as an ambigram, for instance, as opposed to, say, CELERY or ARTHUR, or MOBY GRAPE. But after a while, when I came up with a particularly successful one, my wife and I began saying, "That's one for the book."

THE EMERGENCE OF AMBIGRAMS

I was stunned when I bought a copy of *Omni* magazine in November of 1979 and found that the Games column had been devoted to the dramatically innovative work of a young computer science graduate student at Stanford University named Scott Kim. Scott had designed a number of words that could be read the same both right side up and upside down. He called them "inversions."

Bob Petrick and I had referred to our invertible designs with the comparatively pedestrian term "upside-down-words." But it wasn't the terminology that caused my stomach to flip upside down; for years I had assumed that I had originated the phenomenon, and that Bob and I were the only people in the universe who were creating these things.

Scot Morris, the games column editor at *Omni*, had invited readers to try their hand at creating what he referred to as "designatures." I sent in several of my ambigrams and was further astounded a couple of months later, when the readers' work was published, to find that there were several people dabbling in this "unique" area.

While I was hugely envious of Scott's public debut, my judgment was that most of the pieces *Omni* had published were not up to my standards of readability and attractiveness. I had perhaps only a dozen ambigrams that I considered to be of publishable quality and that had some appropriate reason to be ambigrams, so it was clear to me that if I had a book in my future, it was years away. Scott's book *Inversions* was published in 1981 and included some beautiful pieces that I greatly admired.

One of the people whose names were associated with Scott Kim and *Omni* and unusual approaches to the design of words was Douglas Hofstadter, whose Pulitzer Prize–winning book *Gödel, Escher, Bach* dealt with, among other things, mathematics, symmetry, and pattern in art. It was Doug who coined the term "ambigram."

Still unsure of what formats and venues were right for ambigrams, in the early 1980s I commissioned the construction of two large turntables, on the front of which were silk-screened the "philosophy" and "infinity" ambigrams. These wall-hung pieces would turn the ambigrams at 1 rpm, allowing the observer a more passive role in the relationship with the ambigram. And I began to create a body of work that represented my investigations of the relationships between yin/yang, the infinity symbol, the normal bell curve, wave patterns, and helixes. There were a few paintings, but I was too insecure about my inexperience with painting to depend on that medium. Most of the pieces were constructions of one kind or another, which I was able to create myself, while others required that I commission the services of a neon sign maker, a glass etcher, or an automobile body shop. A number of these pieces appear in this edition of *Wordplay*. When I began teaching typography at Moore College of Art in Philadelphia, I was invited to show this work in the faculty gallery.

A publicist I knew got some coverage of the show on the local ABC television station. The spot paid particular attention to the ambigrams. Then a few months later, the producers of *Good Morning America* decided they'd like to expand and air that piece. Some New Age–type publishers in California saw it and contacted me about doing a book. At the prospect of publishing a book, I began creating new ambigrams—not here and there as time allowed, but as the primary focus of my day, even as we worked on the terms of a contract. Ultimately those negotiations broke down, but by that time the book had become a reality in my mind and I began earnestly looking for a publisher.

I survived the requisite number of discouraging interviews with publishers and compiled a respectable collection of rejection letters before Doug Hofstadter sent me to Ann Freedgood, an editor he thought would be interested. Ann pointed out that what the book needed was text, in addition to the ambigrams. A couple of years later, in 1992, *Wordplay* was published.

While I was writing the text for Wordplay in 1990/91, an interesting challenge arose. The *Omni* articles had revealed that there were several people making ambigrams. One of them, Doug Hofstadter—whose area of study involves, among other things, the way the human mind works and the eyes see, and how they conspire to read language—initiated "the grid project." He asked the six most accomplished ambigram artists to each create an ambigram, keep it under wraps, and then challenge the other five to create one of the same word. The finished grid would theoretically establish whether we all developed similar structures for a given word or whether alternate approaches were possible. I had recently finished the "electricity" ambigram (p. 67) and thought that it would be suitable for Doug's grid. In retrospect, I think it may have been one of the easiest in the group. Although the project never reached a conclusion, all six of us did submit challenge words. Whenever I think that it may be impossible to render a word in ambigrammatic fashion, I should remind myself of David Moser's challenge, "jazz." That and Scott Kim's two-word brain-buster "me/you" each took me uncountable hours to solve. Probably hundreds of trial-and-error sketches and developmental drawings. When one has been challenged in the area of one's own specialty, it's a great example of how competition can spur creativity and accomplishment.

My solutions to "grid project" challenges by Bob Petrick ("bewitched"), Scott Kim ("me/you") Doug Hofstadter ("photograph"), and Lefty Fontenrose ("Picasso").

It takes about a year for a book to go from the author to the publisher and through the publishing process to the bookstores. And while I was happy to take a break from ambigrams for a while and get back to my other careers as a freelance graphic designer and graphic design teacher, I did entertain the fantasy that *Wordplay* would suddenly change my life and soon I'd be a full-time ambigram artist. A few commissions did come my way, but it really didn't work out the way I had envisioned it.

Back in the beginning, I had found that ambigrams were a tough commodity to sell. But having people request them wasn't exactly easy either, since more often than not, words would prefer to remain their unidirectional selves.

There were a few ambigrams that hadn't made the cut for inclusion in the first edition of *Wordplay*. But a year after it was published, I found a use for them at the third congress of the International Society for the Interdisciplinary Study of Symmetry. (In order to help conserve the Earth's dwindling supplies of syllables and ink, it's known as ISIS-Symmetry.) And some of those have now found a home in this book.

Now that I had fully explored my personal version of Taoism using a medium that had grown out of graphic design, it seemed that my ambigram career might be complete. After a couple of years of career confusion, I decided that it was time to commit to painting. The subjects of almost all my paintings are still words, and still the same ideas that inspired ambigrams. And so several of the pieces I produced between 1996 and 2004 have found appropriate placement in this second edition of *Wordplay.* Some of those paintings—most notably, the figure/ground illusions—are the direct descendants of ambigrams.

In the meantime, without my really being aware of it, ambigrams had snuck their way back into my life.

Several months after *Wordplay* was first published, I got a nice letter from a math teacher named Dick Brown. Dick had a copy of the book and, like many who are involved with math and physics, he was quite interested in the symmetrical precision of ambigrams. And like others who have been bitten by the ambigram bug, he was trying to design his own name ambigrammatically—or maybe ambigramathematically. He needed some pointers and I helped him out a bit.

Richard G. Brown

A few years later Dick got back in touch with me, explaining that his son Dan was working on a project and would really like to have an ambigram of the words "Angels & Demons." I was immediately intrigued by the idea, as one of my favorite M. C. Escher prints is *Circle Limit IV* (a tesselation of angels and devils).

When I mentioned that to Dick, he told me that Escher had been an acquaintance of his. The "degrees of separation" circle tightened so quickly that there was not even the slightest hesitation: I agreed to the project right away. I talked to Dan soon after, and his enthusiasm for

M. C. Escher, *Circle Limit IV.*
Woodcut, 1960.

his project and my ambigrams gave me plenty of energy to meet the challenge.

And it was quite a challenge. Some words almost beg to be ambigrams (but not enough!). Some words may look daunting, but then yield to my coercion with little resistance. Some prove to be impossible, either for years, or perhaps even forever. And sometimes, as was the case with "Angels & Demons," it's only my enthusiasm and stubbornness that carry me through to a solution. It was the links to M. C. Escher, the most direct influence on my ambigrams, that fueled me.

It wasn't long until Dan was on the phone again. He told me that the "Angels & Demons" ambigram was to appear as the cover title of his next novel, and he'd decided that what the book really needed were some ambigrams as part of the plot. All our conversations to date had been by way of e-mail and the phone, but we decided we'd better get together to plan our strategy. I invited Dan and his wife, Blythe, down to our weekend house in the woods.

Dan wanted to see as much of the work I'd ever done as I could show him. He looked at paintings, drawings, and, mostly, ambigrams that hadn't been included in *Wordplay,* which he seemed to have practically memorized. We had a very enjoyable weekend as Dan and Blythe quickly seemed like old friends.

Not much time passed before I heard from Dan again. He wondered if it would be possible to create ambigrams of the words *earth, air, fire* and *water.* Could they be done in a style that was sort of ancient looking, maybe a bit creepy, and maybe sort of like the style of the *A&D* ambigram? He wanted each of the four words separately, *and* worked together into a unit. And how about the word "Illuminati"? And could they all be in the same style? Thinking that such a demanding project had little hope of succeeding, but certainly under the spell of Dan's enthusiasm, I promised to give it my best shot.

It's a handy little secret that if a word resists my attempts to make an ambigram out of it, then a gothic blackletter style (often incorrectly referred to as "Old English") is often a successful last resort. The style is somewhat familiar to anyone who's ever seen the masthead of a newspaper, the church bulletin, or certain Grateful Dead or heavy-metal album covers, and yet many of the individual letters, and parts of letters, are quite unorthodox in comparison to most of the typestyles we regularly see. This combination of familiarity and unfamiliarity allows for significant letter manipulation. Ancient? Sort of. Creepy? Sure. Just ask Guns N' Roses or Black Sabbath.

Ordinarily, I'd say the odds in favor of being able to comply with a

request for several specific ambigrams in the same style, both individually and grouped, would be infinitesimally tiny. But the combination of the Escher connection, Dan's enthusiasm, the relative simplicity of the four words and the familiarity of the grouping, the manipulability of black-letter style, and my own stubbornness proved to be the right combination. I was able to do it. Dan was ecstatic.

It was really a kick to have my work be a part of a very exciting popular novel. And certainly an amazing honor to have the main character named for me. And life went on. Time went by, and another Dan Brown book came along—a kind of sequel to *Angels & Demons*, starring the same guy! A Harvard professor of

named

who could probably decode the symbology hidden in those eight glyphs in short order.

And then everything went crazy. Millions of people read *The Da Vinci Code*. It was everywhere in the popular media. Thousands of people went to Dan's Web site and read about not only *The Da Vinci Code*, but *Angels & Demons,* too, and ambigrams, and a lot of them came to my Web site.

When *Wordplay* had gone out of print in 1994, I bought a thousand copies from the publisher, at cost (an excellent value!). I had been selling them from my Web site for nine years at the rate of a few every month. Suddenly, in 2004, I sold almost one a day. The supply dwindled rapidly. A second edition seemed mandatory, especially to Dan, who put me in touch with his agent,

who introduced me to my editor, Becky Cole, at Broadway Books. And you and I have them to thank for the fact that you're reading this.

DAJ78ROWAJ... The most recent chapter brings Dick Brown back into the story. Dick asked me to create a Dan Brown ambigram for Dan's birthday. I had tried any number of times to create a Dan Brown ambigram, with no success. But remembering Dan's love of the Fibonacci series, I was able to spell out his name using those magical numbers in sequence.

Since *Angels & Demons* escorted ambigrams into so many zillions of homes around the world, the demand for ambigrams has been not only gratifying, but thrilling and absolutely overwhelming. Although it's still true that every word or name will not submit to becoming an ambigram, it seems that I still find new ways to create them. Or maybe there have just been enough requests that a good number have worked out well. Some of my favorites are reproduced on the next couple of pages.

Mark Mangold, New York.

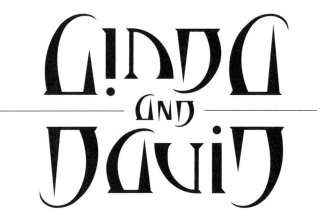

Linda Robertson and David Waxman, Florida.

Elisa Fleischer and Kevin Hotaling,
Massachusetts.

186

Gary Mraz, Studio Voodoo, California.

Mark Willie, Pennsylvania.

Vestnik Znaniya (Herald of Knowledge), to my knowledge, the first Russian ambigram. Commissioned by Raphael Baron, California.

Matt Nolan, Massachusetts.

Crown Vantage Paper Company, Pennsylvania.

John Jensen, Jensen Knives, California.

Media Arts Department, Drexel University, Pennsylvania.

Norman and Rina Indictor, New York.

How a Word
Becomes an Ambigram

Philosophy is written in this grand book—I mean the universe—which
stands continually open to our gaze, but it cannot be understood unless
one first learns to comprehend the language and interpret the characters
in which it is written.

Il Saggiatore, Galileo Galilei

As a professional logo designer and lettering artist, I have two
primary requirements of an ambigram: it should be readable
and it should be attractive. Those factors are not altogether
different: the components of visual attractiveness are, in fact, the characteristics that result in easy readability.

All contemporary typefaces are descendants, to one degree or another, of the letters that Roman designers developed to accompany their
architecture. A couple thousand years later, we still consider both to be
classics. Nobody has done it better. Granted, I take extreme liberties
with classic letterforms. But once the structure of an ambigram has
been determined, I try very hard to imbue that structure with the principles of traditional typography.

Beyond the physical characteristics that render an ambigram attractive and readable, there is a spiritual component that adds a layer of

beauty: an ambigram reaches its greatest potential when there is a resonant relationship between the word, its meaning, and the duality of its "ambi-graphic" representation—an ambigram can then provoke thought beyond a mere appreciation of its symmetry.

The development of an ambigram begins with exploration and play, taking place as doodling in a sketch book or on a layout pad. It's very important, if not critical, to establish an open and relaxed state of mind. All rules, conventions, traditions, and judgments are best left behind in the early stages of trying to accomplish something creative and original.

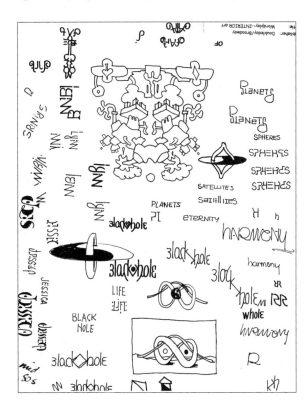

There's nothing special about what's on this page from my sketchbook. But it's pretty typical. There's stuff going every which way (which is sometimes helpful in discovering the ambigrammability of a given word). Much of it's related, much of it's random. I make no attempt at this stage to produce anything that's beautiful, and there's really nothing very good-looking there. And I don't worry much about readability, either. What's happening is open-ended exploration and playfulness. There must be a little judgment operating on some level of not-very-consciousness, because if I see something that looks like it has potential, then I'll either circle it and keep exploring, or I'll get off at that exit and see where it leads.

Typically, I might ponder a number of ideas within a general category—more often than not a subject related to the physical sciences, and its relationship to natural opposites and balances, or issues that the yin/yang symbol might bring to mind, for example, the universal force of electromagnetism and some related concepts: positive and negative, north and south polarities, and so on. I might play with the words *electricity, electron, magnet, magnetic,* and *magnetism, polarity, polar, polarized,* and so forth. All of these mental gymnastics seem to me to be a kind of graphic artist's philosophical self-indulgence, and so words that make up the vocabulary of philosophy would be on my mind as well.

In order to save the time, effort, and the continual disorientation of turning my pad of layout paper upside down, I have become fairly proficient at writing upside down and backward. Each letter is written, in the beginning, in a single pen stroke and in straightforward capital letters.

If a word is likely to work as an ambigram, it almost always depends on some letters being the natural reverse of either themselves, or of other letters. These provide support for the letters that require more distortion and manipulation and might, out of context, be difficult to read. In the word *philosophy*, the *oso* in the middle is a promising sign, as are the *h*'s near either end. The *a* and *v* would be a natural starting point in the word *gravity*. In *magnetic*, the *n* in the middle will work, but nothing else looks helpful right away.

Let's follow the development of the "philosophy" ambigram. I now have the *oso* and the *h*'s, so I need to concentrate on making a *p* that, when reversed, could read as a *y*, and an *il* that could function as a *p*.

First the *p–y* situation. Nothing too obvious here, but I do know that a lowercase *y* can be drawn with a loop at the bottom that might form the protruding bowl of the P, and since the *y* comes at the end of the word, perhaps the loop can be somewhat exaggerated in size. This would form the most important characteristic of a *p*, and as the *p* is the initial character, the exaggeration could allow it to be bigger than the other letters, as an initial capital letter often is. Now the upside-down P offers no suggestions for the split top that is necessary to create a *y*. But in a more flourished handwriting style the *y* almost necessarily creates a fancier, cursive *p*, and now I see a way of getting the *y* to work: a script capital *p* would conceivably have some extraneous material to the left of the main stroke, and by continuing the round stroke of the *p*

through and beyond the backstroke, I have created a reasonably credible *y*.

Making the *il* into another *p* may be a bit more difficult. Not only do I have to make both *p*'s believable within the same design, but I also have to make one letter into two letters, and vice versa. In a case like this, I have to look at individual strokes, not just whole letters. There are two main, vertical strokes in the *il* and a subordinate horizontal stroke. In some forms of the letter *p* there is one predominant vertical with a subordinate vertical attached to it by two connectors, one of which is often minimized in typeface design and sometimes even omitted. And since an *i* in its lowercase form is shorter than an *l*, maybe the *p can* be made from an *i* and an *l*.

Things seem to be working out fairly well, but note that all the manipulations I've been through have guided us toward lowercase forms, whereas I started out with all capital letters. Designing an ambigram is not like designing a typeface. In the design of a typeface, each letter must perform well, functionally and aesthetically, on either side of every other letter in the alphabet. I call this an open system. An ambigram is a closed system. The letters that are drawn for one specific ambigram may not even be recognizable outside the context of that ambigram. This allows the artist significant latitude beyond the rules of everyday typography. For instance, it might be necessary to mix capital and lowercase forms. Nevertheless, readability will be best served if I can avoid breaking any more rules than necessary.

At the moment I have.

PHILOSOPHY

I'm getting there, but it's still not exactly easy to read or particularly attractive. It looks a little like Greek, with some letters recognizable and others not, but while that may be appropriate to the origins of the word (*philos:* love + *sophia:* wisdom), it's not much help in achieving readability in English. Even though it means sacrificing those very important and easy-to-read *h*'s, I think I'm going to have to try moving to all lowercase. The *oso* is great because it works just as well in lowercase. I just have to get an upside-down lowercase *h* that also looks like a right-side-up lowercase *h*. Fortunately, we're in luck. Those earlier decisions that led us toward more cursive, slightly flourishy forms have created a format within which a more cursive, slightly flourishy *h* will be right at home.

Now, I'm in business. I've established the skeletal structure of the design. All that remains between here and a finished ambigram is a decision on style. It is here that critical judgment will determine the readability and attractiveness of the design. In most ambigrams, the necessary manipulations leave a fairly narrow range of stylistic choices. But the eventual style has to be found by trial and error. The way to discover what works, and what works best, is to try a bunch of things that don't work, or don't work as well as I might hope. On occasion the basic structure of an ambigram works so simply and so well that a greater range is afforded, and in that event I try to instill a stylistic flavor appropriate to the meaning of the word. Rarely, as in the case of the "electricity" design on page 67, an almost pictorially symbolic style will actually help the readability and success of the ambigram.

Normally adjacent letters don't touch, but if I'm going to make a convincing *p* out of the *il* pair, a cursive style, with at least those letters connected, will help a lot. The fact that the *il* and *p* combination depends on the traditional placement of thicker and thinner strokes, combined with the fact that some weight variation is natural to a cursive lettering style, and finally, the fact that weight variation helps in readability—especially where some of the letters are less recognizable than usual—leads to the inescapable conclusion that a monoweight style would be a counterproductive choice. So from here on, all the experimentation uses letterforms that show some variation in weight.

As it turns out, the experiments in which the thick and thin strokes tend toward extremes seem a little more difficult to read, so although the weight variation is important, I'll keep it on, the minimal side.

Once the style has been determined in thumbnail sketch form, it is photographically enlarged—I like to draw the final letterforms at a height of about two to three inches. A tracing of the enlarged sketch provides the basis of a large, very careful and accurate drawing done by hand, with a hard pencil. Until the mid-1990s that drawing would be transferred to inking paper. French curves, oval templates, and other instruments were used to outline the letterforms to ensure smooth, clean edges. But since then, the drawings have been scanned and imported into the graphics program Adobe Illustrator, where finished art is created using vector curves. Either way, only half the ambigram needs to be rendered. That half is duplicated, inverted, and joined to its twin in order to complete the ambigram.

The process begins in the intuitive, illogical, "what-the-heck-let's-try-something-impossible" right hemisphere of the brain. Little by little, as judgment is introduced to ensure readability and guide the aesthetic refinements, the process evolves into an increasingly left-brained activity, concluding in the black-and-white, on-and-off, digital brain of a Macintosh.

Philosophy

ACKNOWLEDGMENTS

There were many people who contributed to *Wordplay*'s existence: Scot Morris, Douglas Hofstadter, Scott Kim, Anne Freedgood, Hal Taylor, Paul Trachtman, David Slavitt, and Chris Bouchard were named in the first edition, and I thank them once again for the invaluable gifts of their time and effort.

I neglected to thank Doug Hofstader in the first edition for his contribution to my "John Langdon" ambigram, and I would like to correct that here. I had not yet ventured into the realm of multiple-word ambigrams and had never created a satisfactory ambigram of "John" or "Langdon." Doug sent me a drawing of his structural solution (below) just when I needed it. One of Doug's most significant contributions to the world of ambigrams has been his seemingly inexhaustible ability to envision yet another way to create them.

The entire field of ambigram art owes a "thank you" to Scot Morris, who brought ambigrams up from underground in the Games column of *Omni* magazine in the 1980s. Scot published Scott Kim's "inversions"—as he called what Hofstadter later named "ambigrams." Subsequently, *Omni* also showcased the work of several more "ambi-grammists" who had emerged from the "wordwork." In the 1990s, the World Wide Web extended awareness of the phenomenon—phenome-nally.

But the early years of the new millennium have brought undreamt-of attention to ambigrams by way of Dan Brown's wonderful novel *Angels & Demons*. It is to Dan that I owe the greatest thanks for his enthusiastic and generous support of my work. Were it not for Dan, it seems unlikely that *Wordplay* would have come around again for an encore. And thank you too, Dan, for writing the foreword to this sec-ond edition. Your contribution is greatly appreciated.

It may have been Dick Brown's acquaintance with M. C. Escher and his appreciation for Escher's work that triggered his interest in my am-bigrams. And so to Dick, with his connection to two people of great im-portance in my life, I extend my heartfelt thanks as well.

Last, I would like to thank the folks who bought *Wordplay* more than a decade ago. And those, too, who have responded to my Web site of-fering of *Wordplay* in the intervening ten years. I wish I could have been in touch with the former group as I have the latter, who ordered the book via e-mail. I have enjoyed meaningful correspondence with many of you. It has been heartwarming and both ambigram- and philosophy-affirming to hear what *Wordplay* has meant in your lives.

Thank you all.

Things are as they appear to be; and they are otherwise.

PERMISSIONS

203

A   NOTE   ON   THE   TYPOGRAPHY

The text of *Wordplay* was set in Minion, an Adobe Original typeface designed by Robert Slimbach, released in 1990. Minion is inspired by classical, old-style typefaces of the late Renaissance, a period of elegant, beautiful, and highly readable type designs.